*Many a trip continues long after movement
in time and space have ceased.*

—John Steinbeck, *Travels with Charley*

< *ii* >

An April Across America

MATTHEW STEVENSON

ODYSSEUS BOOKS

This book is dedicated to my sisters,

Nanette and Julie Stevenson,

who also rode the trains south in many spring times,

and to Winthrop Watson and John Russell,

brothers of a kind.

AN APRIL ACROSS AMERICA Copyright©2006 by Matthew Mills Stevenson

ISBN 10-digit 0-9709133-5-4   13-digit 978-0-9709133-5-7

For information, address: Odysseus Books c/o Pathway Book Service, 4 White Brook Road, Gilsum, New Hampshire 03448. Toll free: 1-800-345-6665. Fax: 1-603-357-2073. E-mail: pbs@pathwaybook.com

Please use the same contact numbers for special or direct orders, group sales, or special promotions, for example, those available to book and reading clubs.

Please visit the book's Web site: www.odysseusbooks.com

To contact the author on any matter, such as to arrange a speaking engagement, please use: matthewstevenson@freesurf.ch.

This book was printed on acid-free paper in the United States. It was edited by Michael Martin and Sandra Costich. Jacket and book design by Al Cetta.

Library of Congress Cataloging-in-Publication Data

Stevenson, Matthew Mills, 1954-
    An April Across America / Matthew Stevenson.
        p. cm.
    Includes bibliographical references and index.
    ISBN-13: 978-0-9709133-5-7 (alk. paper)   ISBN-10: 0-9709133-5-4 (alk. paper)
        1. United States—Description and travel. 2. Stevenson, Matthew Mills, 1954—Travel— United States. 3. United States—History, Local. I. Title.
    E169.Z83S725 2006
    917.3'04931—dc22

                                                                    2006026818

10 9 8 7 6 5 4 3 2 1

Contents

Travels Without Charles:
'to try to rediscover this monster land'

For the last fifteen years, I have lived in Switzerland, worked in Europe, and taken vacations in the United States. For professional reasons, I am sometimes in New York or Washington, with the occasional side trip to Boston or a change of planes in Miami. I've even made it to Alaska, where I watched the start of the Iditarod dogsled race. But mostly my view of America is similar to those airline films shown prior to landing on the East Coast: a collage of the Washington Monument, the Statue of Liberty, and Paul Revere's church tower. During summers, with family in tow, I have followed the script of America-on-five-relatives-a-day, driving between Long Island and Maine, eating roadside meals on picnic tables, explaining to small children why we are "not there yet." Pressed by work or eager to see friends and family, I have rarely ventured west of the Hudson River or east of the Golden Gate Bridge.

< 1 >

When my job in Europe was hard—my sister has a quote: "That's why they call it work"—I promised myself that, when it ended, I would ride my bicycle across the U.S. I even went so far as to download routes from the Internet and study the details of organized tours that offer to carry your bags and tent. The dream was fueled by the *National Geographic Atlas of the World*, which has excellent maps of the American national parks and Civil War battlefields. In the evenings, flipping randomly through the atlas pages, I would weigh the advantages of the northern route—including Chicago, Minnesota, and the Badlands—versus the southern passes, which would let me see three states I have never visited: Kentucky, Tennessee, and Arkansas. I also thought I needed to ride east to west, the path taken when lighting out for the territories, instead of the more logical west to east, which would get the Rockies out of the way on fresh legs and follow the prevailing trade winds down east.

In my European daydreams about American travels, no doubt I had in mind trips taken when I was a child growing up on Long Island. In the 1960s, during the twilight of American passenger railroads, I crisscrossed the country any number of times with my father, who traveled for business and often brought one of his children along for the ride. In 1965, for example, along with my older sister,

< 2 >

Nanette, we took sleepers from Pennsylvania Station, in New York, to Brownsville, Texas, and then rode the Mexican railways to Oaxaca (where we skipped the Zapotec ruins in favor of inspecting the world's oldest tree). A few years later my father and I went from Grand Central Terminal on the *Twentieth Century Limited* to Chicago, and then rode other sleepers to Rock Springs, Wyoming, where we caught a minivan into Grand Teton National Park. Over my desk in Switzerland hangs a reproduction of the Edward Hopper print, *Railroad Sunset*, which shows a lonely switch tower in fading light on the High Plains—a connection, in the Swiss countryside, to earlier journeys along the Columbia River or the desert around Flagstaff.

Alas, when my job actually did end, with a bang more than a whimper, I was too distracted with lawyers and claims to set my bike in the direction of San Francisco. Such were my preoccupations after leaving work that I saw no chance to take two months off and ride my bike west. Nor, in a shorter time, could I connect the dots of the Americans I wanted to see with the lines drawn from Amtrak's national timetable.

I also wanted to travel across America to reconnect with some of its writers. During the boyhood years that I was traveling with my father, I had discovered reading. On the trip to Mexico, I read *Thirty Seconds Over Tokyo*, an account of World War

< 3 >

II air raids, and *Heroes of Conquest and Empire*, a politically incorrect history of Alexander the Great, Kublai Khan, and Gustavus Adolphus. On later trips, I read books linked to the landscape, histories of railroads, and even such industrial-age novelists as Theodore Dreiser, who would be elected the poet laureate of day coaches, should such an honorific ever be awarded. It was also on one of these early trips that I first read John Steinbeck's *Travels with Charley*, his account of driving a camper van in a great circle around America. I had selected it from a school reading list, having first noted its modest length. I loved Steinbeck's description of life on the road in the company of his quixotic poodle, Charley. He begins with an explanation as to why he is going: "I, an American writer, writing about America, was working from memory, and the memory is at best a faulty, warpy reservoir. I had not heard the speech of America, smelled the grass and trees and sewage, seen its hills and water, its color and quality of light.... So it was that I was determined to look again, to try to rediscover this monster land." I do not want to imply any literary similarities between Steinbeck and myself. Sitting in Europe during a winter of discontent, I had shared his feelings about wanting to smell cut American grass. Thus I blocked out several weeks in April, booked a plane to New York, and made my plans to head west. All Huck Finn had to do was ease his

< 4 >

craft into the river, but as he observed, "the raft did seem to go mighty slow."

I decided to take the southern route, even though I knew that would mean missing Chicago, a hub on so many of those earlier journeys. After visiting with my parents in Princeton, New Jersey, my plan was to watch baseball in Baltimore, spend a day in Washington, drive across Virginia to Chapel Hill, North Carolina, fly to Alabama and then drive across Mississippi. From Jackson, Mississippi, I booked a flight to Texas, and then another to California. In between planes in Dallas, I would drive to Waco. After a few days in Los Angeles, I would spend a weekend with family in and around San Francisco. I would do all this in less than two weeks, which friends and some family members thought mad. They would say things like, "Why do you want to go to Mississippi?" but then chastise me for missing New Orleans. I had my private list of people and places to see. When I was done somewhere, I did not plan to linger in the botanical gardens or eat dinner in a fancy restaurant. It might not be my bike tour across the Badlands or include my son Charles as a traveling companion, but at least I would escape Europe in early April and see the cherry blossoms around the Tidal Basin.

< 5 >

Newark, New Jersey:
'death comes for the archbishop'

Leaving Newark International Airport, I took New Jersey Transit from the railroad station at the end of the terminal's monorail. Landing in the U.S. in early April, I was surprised at the barrenness of the trees and the grayness of the landscape. When I left Europe, trees and flowers were blooming. But here I was traveling back to the future of late winter doldrums. On the monorail, I was in the small compartment, about the size of an elevator, with an older man who asked me if he was going in the right direction to get into New York City. I told him how to make the connection and answered another question about where he could find a subway. He had never taken New Jersey Transit from the airport. I could not place the origin of his Spanish accent, so I asked him where he was from. "Cuba," he said, "although I haven't lived there since 1965. Castro threw me out."

I generally do not put much stock in random

< 6 >

travelers' tales. But this man had a life story, which he told directly and with a certain unstated passion. When the Cuban revolution swept across Havana, he had been in Venezuela, studying to enter the priesthood. When he was ordained, he returned to Cuba, where Castro put him in prison. He stayed in jail for a few years, until good fortune put him on a plane to exile in Spain. He worked there as a priest, telling anyone who asked about the horrors of the Cuban revolution. Few were listening, so he moved to Rome and got a job as a functionary in the Vatican. There he met and became friends with Cardinal Karol Wojtyla, later to be known as Pope John Paul II, whom he admired both as a human- ist and as someone who despised Communist revo- lutions. They were friends, but not confidants. I asked him what language they spoke together, and he said "Italian and some Spanish. But we also spoke English." The week earlier, John Paul II had lingered on a public deathbed in Rome, and my new priest acquaintance had traveled to stand in the crowds drawn to the vigil. "I don't have much money," he said, "but I felt I had to be there." After John Paul II died, he had lined up to pass the cof- fin and then had flown home to New York. We were separated in the scramble to buy tickets and get on the correct trains. I was going south, and he was heading to the city. From my platform I could see him lugging his tired suitcase onto the northbound

< 7 >

train, as if framed in a passage from *Death Comes for the Archbishop*, another account of a priest from the Old World seeking redemption in the New. Toward the end there is a sentence: "Men travel faster now, but I do not know if they go to better things."

< 8 >

Princeton, New Jersey:
'this side of paradise'

I arrived in Princeton early enough in the day to ride my bicycle. We all have our indulgences, and mine is to sprinkle vintage racing bikes among houses that I often visit. I have one in Maine, another with my younger sister, Julie, who lives in upstate New York, and this Colnago from Italy with my parents. Usually I go for a ride when I am up early with jet lag. But now I had a free afternoon and decided to ride to the Princeton battlefield and then find a bookstore—a tour I know well.

Princeton is the exception to my conclusion that George Washington was a mediocre general who survived mostly with good luck. During the Revolutionary War, Washington was not present for the victory at Saratoga, and lost most of his other battles with the Redcoats (Long Island, Brandywine Creek, and Harlem Heights come immediately to mind). At Princeton, just beyond the colonial town, he scattered several British regiments, this after his

< 9 >

bold stroke across the Delaware and his capture of Trenton. The battlefield park now straddles either side of a busy county road, and the few markers scattered around the grass fields make it hard to imagine minutemen nipping at the heels of the British Empire. Nor does anything around the colonial village of Princeton echo the sentiments of a French officer, who described the father of America to France's senior military officer:

> I have not yet told you anything of the character of General Washington. He is the most amiable, obliging, and civil man but as a General he is too slow, even indolent, much too weak and is not without his portion of vanity and presumption. My opinion is that if he gains any brilliant action, he will always owe it more to fortune or to the faults of his adversary than to his own capacity.

Before dinner I was back in my parents' retirement village, which is on the edge of Princeton and where the men wear neckties to dinner. My parents moved there in 1999, when they were both 80, needing to live in a community where someone else shoveled the walk and where the residents could gather for meals. Before their move, I knew no one in Princeton and had only passed through the college town. But now I am there often, which nurtures my ambivalent relationship with central New Jersey. On the positive side of the ledger, I love the

< 10 >

bookstores near the campus, the cafés that serve bagels and coffee, and the sense of being in an American university town. The co-op bookstore is the kind of place where you can ask for a biography of Sallust and be told, without reference to a computer, that two are in stock, but only that by Ronald Syme is in paperback. But Princeton is also, as one advertisement used to boast, "an executive environment for achievement," headquarters to numerous corporations, and more frantic than many European cities. The setting for *This Side of Paradise*, the title of F. Scott Fitzgerald's Princeton coming-of-degree novel, now includes a lot of eight-lane highways, Wal-Marts, and those *faux* diners that serve jumbo shrimp.

*   *   *

Fitzgerald, perhaps the most famous Princeton student, never graduated from the university. He passed the summer of 1918 drinking gin and waiting to be sent with the army to France. While gin stayed a feature in his life, he neither descended into the trenches nor returned to college, except in his first novel, in which he describes Princeton as "the pleasantest country club in America." He writes of Anthony Blaine, the undergraduate-as-protagonist, that he was "the product of a versatile mind in a restless generation." That might also

< 11 >

have been a description of Fitzgerald himself, who, in *This Side of Paradise,* takes aim not just at collegiate pretensions (one section is called "The Education of a Personage") but also those of postwar America, enjoying a long weekend of affluence and insouciance. "The great rich nation had made triumphant war," he wrote subsequently of the Great War, "suffered enough for poignancy but not enough for bitterness—hence the carnival, the feasting, the triumph." Still the likes of Blaine and Fitzgerald entered the 1920s with the sense of having "grown up to find all Gods dead, all wars fought, all faiths in man shaken."

A friend of Fitzgerald's at Princeton, Edmund Wilson, wrote of his first novel: "I have said that *This Side of Paradise* commits almost every sin that a novel can possibly commit, but it does not commit the unpardonable sin: it does not fail to live." The same could have been said of Fitzgerald, who met his Jazz Age wife, Zelda, while stationed in Montgomery, Alabama. Later they lived in and around New York and Europe, where as a couple they become known for various sins, notably those associated with alcohol and expensive living. ("We ruined ourselves—I never honestly thought that we ruined each other.") Fitzgerald published numerous short stories to support their glamorous lifestyle. His five full-length novels capture five distinct places of his fleeting adult life, which

< 12 >

ended when he was 44: Princeton, New York City, Long Island, France, and Hollywood. Reading Fitzgerald at various phases of my own life—in high school, at college, in New York, and later in Geneva—I often found myself gazing into a distant mirror, if not of my own life, then at least of the places where I was living.

The town where I grew up on Long Island was Fitzgerald's East Egg. As a boy on my bicycle I could ride past a dilapidated mansion that had belonged to the newspaper magnate Herbert Bayard Swope, where Fitzgerald had come for parties and where it would have been possible for Jay Gatsby to see winking lights on Daisy Buchanan's dock. As Fitzgerald wrote of those lost ambitions:

> His dream must have seemed so close that he could hardly fail to grasp it. He did not know that it was already behind him, somewhere back in that vast obscurity beyond the city, where the dark fields of the republic rolled on under the night.

On trips into New York City, I could pass the gas station where Daisy, driving Gatsby's car, could have killed the service attendant. ("They were careless people, Tom and Daisy—they smashed up things and creatures and then retreated back into their money or their vast carelessness, or whatever it was that kept them together, and let other

< 13 >

people clean up the mess they had made.")

After moving to Europe, I searched in Paris, like many American tourists, for the cafés and literary haunts associated with Hemingway's and Fitzgerald's moveable feasts. But Fitzgerald's presence for me is more immediate along the shores of Lake Geneva. Zelda recovered from several nervous breakdowns in Prangins, about twenty minutes outside Geneva. Scott fictionally describes his and her dark nights in *Tender is the Night*, where there is a brief cry of reason: "Trouble is when you're sober you don't want to see anybody, and when you're tight nobody wants to see you." One of his short stories begins: "Switzerland is a country where very few things begin, but many things end." On weekends driving through Vevey, at the north end of the lake, I am reminded of his passages set here, perhaps in homage to Henry James, who has Daisy Miller pass through town on her Grand Tour of American innocence. But it is hard to imagine Fitzgerald ever happy around Lake Geneva, which he described as "a backdrop of mountains and waters of postcard blue, waters that are a little sinister beneath the surface with all the misery that has dragged itself here from every corner of Europe."

I remember reading *The Last Tycoon*, Fitzgerald's last and unfinished novel, just after we moved in 1991 from New York to Geneva. Toward

< *14* >

the end of his life, Fitzgerald had moved to Los Angeles, as if a character in one of his stories: "Maybe he's gone to Hollywood to go in the movies. They say a lot of lost men turn up there." He failed as a screenwriter ("I just couldn't make the grade as a hack—that, like everything else, requires a certain practiced excellence"), but Hollywood gave him material for his last novel, which I read each morning on a small red train that took me to Geneva from our temporary quarters in the foothills of the Alps. Had Fitzgerald lived, his movie mogul, Monroe Stahr, might now be as celebrated as Jay Gatsby.

The novel ends abruptly, as did Fitzgerald's life. The edition I was reading had facsimile pages from some of Fitzgerald's other manuscripts. What struck me about his changes to the typescript was the attention to detail and the labor that went into his writing. By legend, it seems his books and stories were dashed off between cocktail parties and benders. But to look at his edited manuscripts is to understand his devotion to the craft of writing. A contemporary novelist, John Dos Passos, once visited Fitzgerald on Long Island and later recalled: "When he talked about writing his mind, which seemed to me full of preposterous notions about most things, became clear and hard as a diamond. He didn't look at landscape, he had no taste for food or wine or painting, little ear for music except

< 15 >

the most rudimentary popular songs, but about writing he was a born professional."*

* * *

At dinner in Princeton with my parents, I returned to one of my standby conversational set pieces: where will our children someday go to college? My parents are of that World War II "greatest generation" for whom the dividing line between wealth and poverty lies with a university degree. At the same time, they are neither boosters for Princeton ("full of binge drinking and casual sex") nor American colleges in general ("overpriced, not enough Homer"). During the visit, my father referred often to an article that had run in *The Atlantic Monthly*, "Lost in the Meritocracy: How I traded an education for a ticket to the ruling class," an account of Princeton's obsession with success. Living in Europe, where many universities look like council flats, I tend to wax sentimental about the liberal arts, even if in my freshman year I repeatedly had to endure Marx and Sartre in English, psychology, and history classes. In the 1970s, I think universities taught the unreadable Herman Hesse

---

* About writing, he never had the insouciance of his friend Ring Lardner, Jr., who once got out of a taxi and scattered the manuscript of a story. A friend collected the pages, but found two were missing. Lardner, however, was unfazed, remarking: "Makes no difference, it's for *Cosmopolitan*."

< 16 >

in gym classes, and I agree with Woody Allen as Alvy Singer, who advised Annie Hall "never take a class where you have to read *Beowulf*." But that does not solve the university question for my children, especially my oldest daughter, Helen, who is a year away from making her decision.

Helen has grown up in Switzerland and attended the local public schools, in which French is the primary language. She started German in the third grade, and passed out of English, even though she writes it, at times, with phonetic simplicity (I have run across words like "cauf" in her letters). In Switzerland, the liberal arts are taught in *collège*, between ages 15 and 18, after which a limited number of students go to university, which is more like an American graduate school. Every time I discuss with her the possibility of going to school in America, she looks at me as if I were proposing one of those semesters at sea. For the proper context, imagine telling a U.S. high school senior, of Romanian origin, who has gotten good grades, that now she should think about going to college in Bucharest.

Pressing the case of American liberal arts, I took Helen last summer to visit colleges that happened to lie on the route of our summer vacation. We started with New York and Columbia universities, detoured to Georgetown, and then sampled a number of colleges in New England, including Harvard, Colby, and the University of Maine. Many seemed a

< 17 >

variation on the paradise of Princeton; I would have matriculated at any of them, enchanted by the idea of spending the next four years reading and writing papers. At Harvard we inspected the room once shared by Al Gore and the actor Tommy Lee Jones. In Orono, we found out that the University of Maine ranks "number one in the country" for on-campus Saturday night activities. (Who does all this college ranking?) Of the courses or professors my daughter might encounter, most of the campus presentations said little. The emphasis seemed to be on careers launched and connections offered, not to mention wireless connection in the lounges or midnight buffets in the library. In short, American colleges sounded like Flaubert's sentimental education. I had got the impression that American universities have become an extension of those alumni cruises, where you can tour Renaissance Italy or Greek islands in the company of liked-minded travelers.*

* Flaubert describes Frédéric Moreau telling his family that he intends to live in Paris, to which his mother asks:

"What would you do there?

"Nothing!"

Surprised by his manner, Madame Moreau asked him what he wanted to become.

"A minister!" retorted Frédéric.

< 18 >

The Babe Ruth Museum, Baltimore:
'better than the Louvre'

I left Princeton Junction the next day at noon, in time to connect in Trenton to the Amtrak regional train that stopped in Baltimore. A group of friends from around the East Coast had tickets for a baseball game at Camden Yards, officially known as Oriole Park. I had picked the place for the rendezvous, the Babe Ruth Museum, which is in a townhouse near both the stadium and the tavern over which George Herman Ruth grew up—until his exasperated parents sent him to St. Mary's School for wayward boys. The young Babe was uncontrollable, but never unpleasant, and a superb baseball player. When he left school to play professional baseball, one of the priests who had nurtured him, Brother Matthias, said: "You will make it, George," and he did, of course, first with the minor-league Orioles, and later with the Boston Red Sox and the New York Yankees. Between the ages of 32 and 37, Ruth, according to one biographer, "put on

< 19 >

the finest sustained display of hitting that baseball has ever seen," averaging 50 home runs, 155 RBIs, and batting .354.

From the museum, I sent my wife a postcard, informing her it was "better than the Louvre." In fact, the real Babe will never get into the display cabinets. After he retired, he once quipped that he should write one account of his life for adults and another for children. Clearly the kid version was on display in Baltimore, which includes newsreels of the Babe visiting sick children and calling home runs in the World Series. But as our group of five friends wandered around the museum, I whispered the adult biography to anyone who was nearby.

The man whom Yankees owner Colonel Rupert called "Babe Root" was, according his biographer Robert Creamer, "a guileless child." He continued: "He was so alive, so attractive, like an animal or a child: ingenuous, unself-conscious, appealing." He quotes Frank Graham who said: "He was a very simple man, in some ways a primitive man. He had little education, and little need for what he had." Tom Meany said he had the supreme self-confidence of the naïve. There is a picture in the museum of Ruth shaking hands with President Warren Harding on a hot day at the Washington ballpark, but missing from the caption is the Babe's greeting to the President: "Hot as hell, ain't it Prez?" He was

< 20 >

a notorious womanizer who used to tell his team-mates discreetly that he was "going to see a party." There is the famous quote to a journalist who asked Ruth's roommate:

"You room with him. What's he like when you're alone with him?"

"I don't room with him," the roommate answered. "I room with his suitcase."

Once when the Babe was celebrating an important victory in his hotel suite, the hotel refused to send up a piano. So Ruth simply bought one for the party. Later, perhaps waxing sentimental over the chords, Creamer tells that "Ruth climbed on a chair, a beer in one hand and a sandwich in the other, and shouted, 'Any girl who doesn't want to fuck can leave now.'"

< 21 >

Oriole Park at Camden Yards:
'America's most costly hostage crisis'

Like any group of guys going to a ball game in Baltimore, we ate dinner along the renovated Inner Harbor, which is proof to the world that the city has come to life after suffering decades of urban decay. We sat outside at a table that overlooked the broad stripes and bright stars of Fort McHenry and ordered beer from a Lithuanian waitress—without quoting from the Babe. The excitement of the evening was to see Oriole Park, the stadium built in the early 1990s and credited, along with the inner harbor redevelopment, with Baltimore's revival. Only one of us had been to a game there, but as we ate Tex-Mex and watched tourists stroll along the waterfront, everyone at the table had an opinion on whether new stadiums do more for the rise or the fall of modern American cities.

My friend of thirty years, Winthrop Watson, a banker in both New York and Washington, surprised me by saying that Baltimore's renaissance

< 22 >

was an illusion, confined to the downtown areas near the tourist attractions. Beyond Camden Yards and the like, he felt Baltimore had lost jobs and seen an increase in violent crime. Another friend at the table, Tom Leonard, who has worked to redevelop Harrisburg, Pennsylvania, for more than twenty years, said subsidized towers, restaurants, and stadiums look good to visitors, but rarely spill over into sustained development. He said that Baltimore is still struggling. Washington eats from the trough of federal handouts, and New York, to use Tom Wolfe's expression, lives off the golden crumbs that fall from the cutting boards of Wall Street. But Baltimore, beyond the Inner Harbor, does not even live off the fumes of H. L. Mencken. Russell Baker describes the Depression-era Baltimore in *Growing Up* as "miles and miles of row houses, all with red brick façades, flat rooftops, four or five marble or sandstone steps. It was a triumph of architectural monotony." Since then, the city's population has declined by about 300,000. In those days it survived without major-league baseball.

Because it was a rainy April night, Oriole Park was mostly empty. Our $40 seats were located behind the foul pole in right field, further evidence that a family night out to see professional baseball costs around $300. We had only marginal interest in the game, played against the Athletics, and thus spent the evening exploring the stadium, as if we

< 23 >

were architectural historians and not baseball fans. For my part, I liked, but did not love Camden Yards, the first of the inner-city stadiums meant to recapture neighborhood baseball, as has been lost in Brooklyn, Philadelphia, and other cities. Beyond the right-field fence, leaving aside Boog Powell's barbecue stand, is a renovated railroad warehouse, and beyond the terraced gardens in center field is the Baltimore skyline, still as evocative in the evening as it was in the dawn's early light. But Oriole Park is not that cozy—it seats 48,000—and its 72 skyboxes (revenue not shared with anyone) raised my doubts that the then Orioles owner and Washington insider, Edward Bennett Williams, had paid his share of the costs. Yet, behind the grandstands are lounges with sofas, like those you would find in a Hyatt lobby, a far cry from the urinal atmosphere of Yankee Stadium. But watching the Orioles grind out a victory against Oakland, which included a homer hit into Boog's barbecue pit, I sensed that new stadium revivals have more to do with enriching owners and are less concerned about providing a link to the 1930s or the boys of summer.

I began changing my mind about retro-stadiums while writing a review about *Foul Ball*, an account by former Yankee pitcher Jim Bouton, who with a colleague tries to save Wahconah Park in the Berkshires from the wrecker's ball. Local

< 24 >

entrenched interests—the law firm, the newspaper, General Electric, etc.—push for the construction of a new $18-million-minor-league stadium, to be financed with a smoke-and-mirror bond issue, floated to obscure how taxpayers will fund the cost of construction. Bouton believes that Wahconah Park can be saved for about $2 million, but clearly no one would get rich on that—with the exception of the fans, who would then have an independently owned team. While writing about Bouton's efforts to save the old ballpark, I found a book about stadium finance. Andrew Zimbalist, an economist at Smith College, had undertaken much of this research and published it in a book that he had edited, *Sports, Jobs & Taxes: The Economic Impact of Sports Teams and Stadiums,* in which I later went through the invoices paid by Baltimore to redevelop Camden Yards.

Finished in 1992, Oriole Park cost the taxpayers of Maryland $200 million, none of which was paid by the baseball team. All Williams and the Birds had done was threaten to leave town if a new stadium were not built; they agreed to pay $6 million to rent the new ballpark. The annual expense to Baltimore for Oriole Park, including debt service and maintenance, runs about $20 million. According to Bruce W. Hamilton and Peter Kahn, economists who studied its local impact, the new stadium created about 460 jobs locally. But for the

< 25 >

Orioles, the new ballpark meant an additional $23 million in new revenue, cash flow that could be invested in the pumped-up Raphael Palmiero or the bat-corking Sammy Sosa. Hamilton and Kahn estimate that the Orioles enjoy a $9.7-million rent subsidy or that the net cost to Maryland for the stadium is $11 million a year. That works out to $14.70 per capita for every resident of Baltimore. Maybe a price worth paying to live in a city with major-league baseball? But in the last twenty years, America has invested more than $15 billion in all sorts of new arenas and stadiums, always under the guise that they will attract a major-league franchise or keep an existing one from decamping. Jim Bouton refers to this sporting blackmail as "America's most costly hostage crisis," one in which sport is reconfigured as a variation on the oil depletion allowance.

< 26 >

Washington, D.C.:
'unwitting citizens'

I spent only a day in the capital, and most of that was with lawyers. But it pleased me to arrive in the refurbished Union Station, which I remember first seeing on that trip in 1965, where my father, sister, and I briefly got off the train heading south and gazed at the Capitol. An early morning commuter train from Baltimore put me into the Washington station, and I met an editor and friend for coffee under the restored rotunda, a grand hall of polished marble and soaring columns. It prompted me to recall the sad history of Union Station, which was completed in 1903, with as many democratic aspirations as the Congress that is just down the street.

After rail passenger service collapsed in the late 1960s, and Amtrak inherited some of the nation's railway assets, Union Station fell into disrepair. Like many stations, it was dingy, damp, and home to pigeons and to what in those days were called

< 27 >

lowlifes. By comparison, thanks to generous federal subsidies, airports shone with modern innovation. During the 1960s in New York, Pennsylvania Station and its proud eagles were torn down, but Union Station limped along until the administration of President Richard Nixon got the idea to make it the "nation's visitor reception center." The railroad station was shunted into a cramped basement. Perhaps with the goal of making Union Station look like a bus depot, it was done up with those plastic chairs and televisions that cost twenty-five cents for fifteen minutes of air time. Those who took the train were like rats scurrying down holes. Under the once arching dome, the government covered the marble with honeycombed sheet rock that gave Union Station the feel of a mobile home. It was host to a few inaugural balls. Like other federal offices, the station was prone to leaks. It welcomed neither train travelers nor visitors, except those eager to see oversized portraits of President Nixon.

The newly renovated station, in keeping with the age, is largely a mall—the usual concourses of Victoria's Secret and fast-food dispatchers. But the rest of the station shimmers in marble. Even with crowds rushing through it, the rotunda is stately and hushed. The waiting areas for trains still feel like those of Greyhound, but not far from the gates are restaurants and bookstores. While waiting for

< 28 >

my friend, I lingered over an exhibition of World War II photographs. Taken by the Associated Press, they captured in black-and-white the improbable collision of industrial armies at places like Tarawa and the Hurtgen Forest.

Why am I not happier in Washington? I don't know why I have reservations about the city. Visually it is beautiful, and on a spring day such as this one, I could walk along the Mall surrounded by springtime flowers and cherry blossoms. I love the Smithsonian Museum, especially the building devoted to American history. Even on this busy day, I ate lunch there with a curator and college friend who showed me a new exhibit about America in the 1950s. The rooms have a train engine, old cars, buses, memorabilia from Route 66, and even the logo of a motel cabin. It reminded me that, in 1941, FBI Director J. Edgar Hoover had warned, according to one account I read, "that if motels were allowed to proliferate along the highways, citizens would sleep unwittingly on mattresses still warm from 'illicit relations.'" Alas, none of those bedsprings were on display. On other trips to Washington, I have gone running or walking at dawn among the presidential monuments—those celebrating Abraham Lincoln, Franklin Roosevelt, and Thomas Jefferson—an inspirational way to start any morning. But usually by late afternoon, whether from fatigue or jet lag, I find Washington

< 29 >

inaccessible behind an imperial façade.

Today, between meetings, I had a taxi drop me at the new World War II Memorial. On the Mall between the Lincoln Memorial and the Capitol, it consists of an oval of marble pillars around which are engraved the names of the fifty states and the major American battles. The monument cost almost $200 million, and much of the money was raised privately. But the result is banality surrounded by fountains. Surely for $200 million, it is not unreasonable to expect eloquence or at least historical accuracy? Where are the maps of lost convoys? Where are the blunders at Omaha Beach that cost so many lives in the sand? Where is the language of battle, such as that of marine mortar man E. B. Sledge, who writes: "War is such a self-defeating, organized madness the way it destroys a nation's best." Where are the suicidal orders like those given to Russell Davis on Peleliu's Bloody Nose Ridge? Davis recalls: "I didn't worry about death any more. I had resigned from the human race. I only wanted to be as far forward as any man when my turn came." Instead the visitor is served polished marble, a pointless roll call of the states, and the sense that new Washington lives in the world of the old Soviet monumental realism. I was hoping to find the spare elegance of the Gettysburg address; instead it felt as if I had taken a walk in Gorky Park. A temporary exhibit of photographs at Union

< 30 >

Station had said more to me about World War II than $200-million worth of marble.

One of the lawyers I was meeting had his offices in suburban Virginia, and I got there on the underground Metro. My wife and I were in the midst of rewriting our wills, taking note that the older children have lived in Switzerland for fourteen years. For a half hour, literally, I signed away my life, and then my lawyer, Fred Tansill, took me on a driving tour of the neighborhood. I had visited him before, and knew parts of northern Virginia from trips in and out of Dulles Airport. Not long before I had also driven with a friend from Washington to the battlefields at Bull Run, which every year has its flanks turned by suburban enfilade. But Fred wanted to show me estate and other taxes at work in the homeland security industry. By his account, since September 11, millions of square feet of new offices have been built in and around Tyson's Corner, Virginia. We drove past any number of half-built glass office centers. He said more than half of these buildings were to be leased to security contractors, for whom intercepts and wiretaps are the ball bearings in the war on terror. It cast the attacks on the World Trade Center and the Pentagon as preludes to a gold rush—one of those controlled explosions miners use to tap into a lode.

I should have enjoyed dinner more than I did. At the table were some of my favorite people. We

< 31 >

met in a Washington brasserie, close enough to the FBI that I could make a few Hoover jokes. * The dinner company even included a *Washington Post* political reporter, so we had an unimpeachable source to assess the state of the Clintons' marriage or run down the list of those who might have outed Valerie Plame as a CIA operative. The wine was excellent. But I was under the influence of jet lag, which strikes me on the second or third night of a transatlantic trip. By the time I got a second wind, we were taking pictures on the sidewalk and driving out to Falls Church, to spend the night in the house of friends. And the next morning, after a lazy breakfast of fresh berries and strong coffee, three friends and I were in a rental car, heading south to North Carolina.

* The FBI director once testified: "I regret to say that we of the F.B.I. are powerless to act in cases of oral-genital intimacy, unless it has in some way obstructed Interstate commerce."

< *32* >

Searching Virginia
for Stonewall Jackson:
'you must hold your ground, sir'

You could not ask for a more interesting group of friends for a road trip. Behind the wheel was Michael Martin, the editor of a small literary magazine, *Hogtown Creek Review*, who had arranged for the two of us to speak at Duke University. I was in the front passenger seat, flipping through a stack of maps that I had brought from Europe. In the back seat were Winthrop Watson and John Russell, friends of mine since the 1970s who, themselves, had gone to high school together in Greensboro, North Carolina. John, Winthrop, and I had met at the World Series in 1977 and found that we shared many things, in addition to being the same age and liking baseball. John and I had been at Columbia University at the same time, and later all three of us worked for magazines or publishing houses in New York. By the mid-1980s, Winthrop and I were working for banks, and John had graduated from Harvard Law School and was practicing in the

< 33 >

South. But even after I moved to Switzerland, the fraternal bonds persisted. Every week or two, I speak to Winthrop on the phone—to round up the usual suspects in New York sports and politics—and he sees John on trips home to North Carolina.

I wish I had the ability to capture the conversation that spun during the six-hour drive to Chapel Hill. That night I tried to make a list of the topics we touched upon, but reading it later makes it look like the phone log of a call-in radio program: what's wrong with the Yankees' pitching, why didn't Kerry beat Bush, what happened on September 11 (Winthrop had escaped from Ground Zero), how can Americans afford $3-million-dollar houses, why don't banks make money, why is Clinton so friendly with the Bushes, why can't the Jets win a Super Bowl, how did Dean Smith win all those basketball games at North Carolina, is Faulkner really a great novelist, what's it like in Big Sky, Montana, and so on, as we drove south on Interstates 95 and 85. What's nice about a road-trip conversation is that no one can end it by leaving the dinner table, turning on television, or having to catch a flight. What's more, everyone in the car listens, and the sentences get more complex and interesting the longer the trip lasts. John described going to college with Senator John Edwards, referring to him as "Johnny." He explained that while the Democrats didn't win

< 34 >

either South or North Carolina, Edwards made it close in Ohio and Michigan, where otherwise, had he not been on the ticket, women might have drifted toward George W. Bush. Of course, all of us were skeptical of each other's theories, jokes, and observations, but we would have listened to them for hours.

One problem I have with road trips is that I want to stop everywhere. (My wife, by contrast, is an Interstater.) On this occasion, I tipped my hand when John asked if he could see our route south, and I handed him a map labeled "Battlefields of the Civil War with Descriptive Notes," which prompted backseat laughter. When we needed a rest stop, I lobbied for Chancellorsville and, afterwards, a short excursion through the Wilderness and Spotsylvania Court House. I am sure not everyone in the car wanted to turn a six-hour drive into an all-day battlefield tour, but it was high springtime in Virginia, with dogwoods flowering, and the secondary roads off the Interstate rolled through budding forests and fields suddenly coming alive with wheat and corn.

At my gentle prompting we lingered in the Chancellorsville bookshop and watched the Park Service film of the 1863 battle, in which Robert E. Lee and Thomas J. "Stonewall" Jackson, by dividing their forces, managed to prevent a superior force of Union soldiers from penetrating much

< 35 >

to the south of the Rapidan River. A year later, Grant fought two bloody engagements near Chancellorsville in what is called the Wilderness, a dense forest, and at Spotsylvania, where Grant, now commanding the Union army, sent his men over the top in a form of trench warfare. My interest in Chancellorsville centered on the death of Stonewall Jackson, cut down by his own men in the gloaming as he scouted beyond the front lines. In my mind his loss reversed the fortunes of war for the Confederates, as Lee never found a subordinate with the same fortitude and single-minded courage with whom he could sketch battle plans in the dirt. After Chancellorsville, the Army of Northern Virginia never won another major engagement.

Near the visitors' center, where I bought Douglas Southall Freeman's biography of Lee and short stories by Ambrose Bierce, we found an obelisk that marks where Jackson fell to friendly fire. In addition to writing the definitive biography of Lee, Freeman was the grandfather of my good friend, Doug Adler, the editor of the *Richmond Times Dispatch*, and wrote *Lee's Lieutenants*, a three-volume history that tells the story of men like Jackson. When Jackson went forward off the Chancellorsville Pike, according to Freeman, he was attempting to rally his troops for yet another counterattack against confused Union forces:

< 36 >

About 200 yards he rode through shadows and in the uncertain light of a moon still low in the East. He passed Heth's Brigade and then Lane's. In the belief that he could organize quickly a night attack, he sent one staff officer after another to assist in the deployment and to urge Hill to hurry. The spirit of his speech, the sharpness of his commands, was that of a battle still raging.

Before the war, Jackson had been an uninspiring lecturer at Virginia Military Institute. In battle, however, he came alive with instincts for decisive action, as when he cut off the Union advance at First Bull Run. Where we stood, Jackson was not killed but severely wounded in the shoulder and arm, and some days later, after losing his arm to amputation, he died of pneumonia. But where we stood, despite his loss of blood on the battlefield, Jackson never lost his habits of command. As Freeman writes:

> Jackson could not think in terms of his wounds when there was a suggestion of withdrawal. Instantly he was himself—the corps commander—and he raised his head to answer with flashing eye: "You must hold your ground, General Pender; you must hold your ground, sir!"

A year after Jackson's death at Chancellorsville, the Civil War was won and lost in a series of desperate

< 37 >

encounters in the ten miles near Chancellorsville that connect the Wilderness to Spotsylvania Court House. In early May, after crossing the Rapidan River, Ulysses S. Grant wrote to his commander in Washington: "I propose to fight it out on this line if it takes all summer." But as one Grant biographer noted: "In May 1864 Ulysses Grant began a vast campaign that was a hideous disaster in every respect save one—it worked. He led his troops into the Wilderness and there produced a nightmare of inhumanity and inept military strategy that ranks with the worst such episodes in the history." In this overture to the Great War, Grant suffered 20,000 casualties. But unlike his predecessors, he refused to retreat and refit, moving the army slightly east and attacking again at Spotsylvania, which Edwin M. Stanton called: "the bloodiest swath ever cut through this globe." In these engagements the Civil War became battles of attrition.

We got out of the car at what is now called the Bloody Angle. No battlefield I have seen, with the exception of Verdun, is a stronger reminder of the tragedy of war than Spotsylvania. The woods are as thick as those at the Wilderness, but there is also a clearing that the troops called the "mule's shoe," which came to be known as the Bloody Angle. In a macabre way it invites a battle. Trees, like a band of silent spectators, surround the field, which slopes like a dish to the center. On the southern rim is a

< 38 >

trench, what remains of the southern line. Three hundred yards north is a row of pine trees. From here Grant launched his waves of attack. There is little to interrupt the eye from one side to the other except some shrubs and dead trees, and even this vegetation evokes a sense of dying, so many generations after the fighting. Altogether it forms an amphitheater, now empty, for a terrible history, evoking the words of Stephen Crane: "the delirium that encounters despair and death." At the Wilderness and at Spotsylvania, both sides suffered a combined 70,000 casualties, but in the year that followed, the North had more men to lose.

< 39 >

Bull Durham, North Carolina:
'have you heard of Walt Whitman?'

We were spending the weekend in Chapel Hill at the home of John Russell. The house is only a few blocks from the main campus of the University of North Carolina, which we drove around on our way through town. The beautiful red brick buildings and the flowering trees prompted yet another conversation about whether my daughter should go to college in Europe or the United States. "Send her here," John kept saying, "and we can look after her." On the second weekend in April, it was hard to argue with the proposition that a child could do no better for higher education than UNC Chapel Hill. John, himself, had been accepted here and at Yale, and chose UNC and its full scholarship. After that he worked as a book editor, as a partner in a law firm, and as general counsel to a large corporation while at the same time writing several novels and being active in state politics. In Switzerland, my reservation about the University of Geneva is

< 40 >

that it skips the liberal arts in favor of professional qualification. Nor is there a campus like that which we were touring, and Geneva students tend to live at home—missing the bridge between childhood and independent living that a campus life affords. But, as I said to John, North Carolina is a long way from home.

Most of what we did in Chapel Hill was sit on the Russells' gray front porch, sip at longneck beers, skim the *New York Times*, and tell stories. It's how we spent our weekends when all of us were in our twenties and living in New York, and the pattern was familiar to everyone. We even connected with Debbie McGill, another friend from our twenty-something circle, who had also moved home to North Carolina. She and I had been assistant editors together at *Harper's*, during the 1970s and early 1980s, until that incarnation of the magazine had folded. Debbie left for *The Atlantic*, and I spent more than a year looking for a job, until I found one in international banking. Debbie fed us brunch, and then we went walking in a state park. But Debbie knows me well enough to know that what I really wanted to do was drive around Durham. At the end of the afternoon, we went touring, although it was partly just an excuse to reminisce in the car.

When Debbie and I started at *Harper's* in 1978, Lewis H. Lapham, then as now, was the editor-in-

< *41* >

chief, having replaced those who quit when Willie Morris resigned (or was fired) in the early 1970s. The *Minneapolis Star and Tribune* owned the magazine. Their retainers would periodically call in at the offices to assess the cumulative losses of the monthly magazine. *Harper's*, in my tenure, never made money, losing about $200,000 – $300,000 a year. It had a circulation of close to 300,000 and internally was thought to stroke the ego of John Cowles, Jr., who had inherited from his father the *Star and Tribune* and thus America's oldest monthly. Debbie and I read both solicited and unsolicited manuscripts, edited articles, came up with catchy titles, and took writers to lunch, all of which we did with the enthusiasm of those on their first job. In my time, I edited pieces by the likes of George Plimpton, Joseph Epstein, Carlos Fuentes, Ted Sorenson, and Larry Heinemann, and with some of these writers I stayed friends. The *Star and Tribune* folded the magazine in 1981, although subsequently the family of the MacArthur Foundation bailed it out.

In the car, I told Debbie about having recently read *New York Days* by Willie Morris. In our day, Morris was the ghost of *Harper's* past who loomed large over the magazine. As editor in the '60s and early '70s, he had turned over the magazine's pages to the likes of Norman Mailer and other new-journalism writers, who made the fatal error of

< *42* >

stroking their own egos more than that of John Cowles, Jr., who eventually fired Morris. I had never met Morris and was skeptical of his writing. But in an airport bookstore before a long flight, I found his memoir of editing *Harper's* and read it with interest, perhaps more than with pleasure. (Names are dropped early and often: "It was an equally sizeable gathering later that evening at Jean Stein's when Bobby Kennedy and I were there.") Debbie and I had been to several dinners with John Cowles, Jr., and thus I could appreciate Morris's profile of the proprietor: "There was often something wooden about him, stolid and impervious, an absence of emotional feeling, yet with this a curious compulsive quality about ideas and commitments and values. A classmate recalled his nickname at Harvard had been 'Funlover,' since his approach to everything was mainly the opposite." Our nickname for Cowles, Jr., was the White Rabbit, from Alice's Wonderland. I knew what Morris meant when he wrote: "John Jr. and his corps of assistants thrived on meetings, meetings on anything for any purpose." Morris quotes Alfred A. Knopf, the celebrated publisher, when Morris himself became editor at age 32: "It will take more than one man to ruin *Harper's*." But Morris had devoted single issues to Norman Mailer, and Cowles shut it down.

Durham struck me as the butt end of an unfiltered cigarette. Its heyday was the 1940s, when

< 43 >

Hollywood stars like Humphrey Bogart were reciting their lines in between lighting up. On a Sunday afternoon, the downtown was forlorn, and the brick warehouses that had earlier stored tobacco fortunes appeared as dated as slogans announcing that "I'd Walk a Mile for a Camel." Debbie parked so that I could inspect the old ballpark of the Durham Bulls, celebrated in the minor-league epic, *Bull Durham*. The movie deals with the not-unpleasant subjects of baseball and sex, and it stars Kevin Costner, Tim Robbins, and Susan Sarandon, all of whom are looking to go downtown. Demoted from "the Show," or the major leagues, Kevin Costner as Crash Davis is on his way down while phenom pitcher Nuke LaLoosh is on his way up, at least when in the company of Sarandon's Baseball Annie. Crash hits more clichés than sliders, as when he delivers his 'what I believe in' speech to Annie: "Well, I believe in the soul, the cock, the pussy, the small of a woman's back, the hanging curve ball, high fiber, good scotch, that the novels of Susan Sontag are self-indulgent, overrated crap. I believe Lee Harvey Oswald acted alone. I believe there ought to be a constitutional amendment outlawing Astroturf and the designated hitter." He might well have added baseball's antitrust exemption, which allows owners to blackmail fans over moving their teams. But I still found the movie to be a waist-high fastball.

< *44* >

Weeds now cover the infield, and the grandstand is as shabby as I imagine that of Bouton's Wahconah Park. At some point, perhaps to accommodate high school baseball, it looks like someone shortened the outfield fences. I had the feeling even I could hit one out. The raging Bulls sign is gone.* Debbie and I also went by the new Durham Bulls minor-league stadium, built, of course, with generous local subsidies. I convinced the usher to let me look around and watch a few Toledo Mud Hens hit. In most every way, the stadium is a scaled-down version of Camden Yards, which is not surprising as the same architectural firm designed both ballparks. Build it, and tax dollars will come.

We ended our Sunday drive on the Duke campus, where the next day I spoke about the confluence of literature and politics, a high-minded subject for a talk that attracted few followers. As Michael Martin and I arrived mid-day at the library, we saw hundreds of students streaming out of the building. A fire alarm had sounded. When the crisis passed, no one sounded a similar bell to send everyone back into the library or to our

---

* One home run against the scoreboard mascot prompted the famous exchange between the catcher Crash and Nuke:

Nuke: God, that sucker teed off on that like he knew I was gonna throw a fastball!

Crash: He did know.

Nuke: How?

Crash: I told him.

< 45 >

lecture. It was mid-April, near the end of the second semester, and the quad was alive with Frisbees and tank tops. Hence, as is true of a lot of writing—be it about politics or literature—we were speaking to ourselves, and I missed the chance to quote from Nuke when Annie reads him poetry and he gasps: "Ooh, I've heard of stuff like this." "Yeah?" she answers. "Have you heard of Walt Whitman?" To which Nuke responds: "No. Who's he play for?"

Afterward, Michael and I wandered the campus of gothic gray stone buildings—which is why it is described as the Princeton of the South. Beyond the central campus are tennis courts, various auditoriums and stadiums, formal gardens, inns, and small mansions that house the most obscure academic pursuits—along the lines of Tibetan studies—and dormitories that reminded me of charming hotels of the world. Could I imagine any of my children at school here? I know Duke is a world-class university, richly endowed, thanks in part to my friend Sallie Shuping Russell's success at managing its endowment. I know the university's research to be superb, and I am sure the professors are thoughtful; the two I met, from the department of political science, were. But Duke presents higher education as a learning factory, in which student tuition is needed to move an assembly line that pays administrators' salaries, funds sabbaticals, and constructs arts centers. In this Faustian bargain,

< 46 >

the local economy gets about $200,000, spread over four years, and undergraduate students get a bachelor's degree, which lets them advance their life token to Boardwalk or Marvin Gardens and enjoy easy living. Time-shares are sold on the same principle.

< 47 >

Birmingham, Birmingham:
'greatest city in Alabam'

To get from Durham to my next stop in Birmingham, I decided to fly, having found a $99 fare on the Internet and because Amtrak's *Crescent* only left North Carolina in the middle of the night. Naturally, I changed planes in Atlanta, watched 90 minutes of the Weather Channel, ate a plastic chicken sandwich wrap, and, on arrival, checked into an Embassy Suites Hotel, where the view from my room was a sultry atrium bar. I wondered what Director Hoover would have thought of such accommodation. I had never been to Birmingham and was there for meetings, made notable by lunch on the second day when I was taken to a roadside barbecue stand and given ribs and cole slaw, which are unknown in Europe. But I also had hopes of seeing where in Birmingham the Civil Rights movement had collided with Bull Connor's fire hoses and police dogs, a confrontation that laid bare the rabid face of segregation.

< *48* >

As I was born in 1954 and was fourteen when Martin Luther King was assassinated, I was once, if not twice removed from the battles over racial equality. I never saw King in person. I later met, but only in passing, a number of his close aids: Ralph Abernathy, Jesse Jackson, and Bayard Rustin, with whom I had lunch.* I grew up in a white suburb outside New York, in which there were few racial tensions. Sometime during my early childhood the word *Negro* was phased out, and my mother often corrected my father for never quite keeping up with the linguistic times. During the Newark race riots in the summer of 1964, my grandmother found in *Life* magazine the picture of a dead rioter lying in a pool of blood, noticed his name in the caption, and recalled that she had taught him in the 1950s when she was substitute teaching. In 1968, my mother took me out of school so that I could meet Robert Kennedy at a tea held by the League of Women Voters. Only about fifteen or twenty women were gathered in a neighbor's living room, and he was not only gracious to me, the only boy in the room, but spoke eloquently about King, who had just died. Then a few weeks

* Taylor Branch describes him in the 1950s: "Rustin was an internationally respected pacifist, as well as a vagabond minstrel, penniless world traveler, sophisticated collector of African and pre-Colombian art, and a bohemian Greenwich village philosopher.... He would have taxed the imagination of Dickens or Hugo to invent him." But when I met him he wore a suit and spoke softly about his years with King.

< 49 >

later, Kennedy himself was dead, in a pose not unlike the picture in *Life* magazine that had introduced me to violence in America.

After King was killed, I read a number of biographies of his life. In addition, on other travels over the years, I had visited several places associated with the Civil Rights movement and his life, including the Woolworth's counter in Greensboro, North Carolina, and King's birthplace and Ebenezer Baptist Church in Atlanta. On this trip the landscape of the confrontation in Birmingham eluded me. Most of my meetings, plus the hotel, were outside the downtown part of the city. I did drive there, but glass office towers now shadow the blocks where Connor confronted demonstrators, and few plaques commemorate such an ugly history. Nevertheless, it pleased me that Birmingham, a hub of banks, insurance companies, and retail outlets, now has the face more of George Babbitt than of George Wallace.

In this case, to fill in the blanks, I retreated to *Parting the Waters: America in the King Years 1954–63* by Taylor Branch, who won the Pulitzer Prize for his 924-page effort. En route I read a copy that I hauled in my carry-on luggage, weighed down because of the length and sometimes the prose. A former contributor to *Harper's*, he portrays King during the years of desegregation as gifted both in the pulpit and in positioning the movement

< 50 >

through a series of nonviolent encounters: from the Montgomery bus boycott ("My feet is tired but my soul is rested") to the freedom rides ("Most of the bus stations were located in parts of town where the Supreme Court and Gandhi were never discussed"). In Birmingham, King knew Bull Connor's reputation for what Branch calls "bareknuckled police tactics." But the prospect of violence did not scare King, who had been attacked or imprisoned on a number of occasions: "If it comes, we will surface it for the world to see."

From Birmingham, I planned to drive about four hours to Oxford, Mississippi, which was home to William Faulkner and where James Meredith integrated the University of Mississippi. My European road maps suggested that a highway from Birmingham to Memphis (passing close to Oxford) was nearing completion, and I plotted at the car rental agency how I could connect with Interstate 78 until my eye spotted Tuscaloosa off this four-lane trail. To get there would mean driving south by about forty miles, and then I would have to take more back country roads through Mississippi to reach Oxford. In exchange I would see the University of Alabama—probably not the school for Helen—but the alma mater of my boyhood hero, New York Jets quarterback Joe Namath. By his own account, *I Can't Wait Until Tomorrow... 'Cause I Get Better Looking Every Day*, in addition to

< 51 >

playing football, Namath spent his college years chewing on a toothpick and napping in classes: "I was a triple-threat man in college. On the football field, I was a double-threat." When he left Alabama to sign a $427,000 contract with the Jets, he was fifteen credits short of his degree.

I was not sure of my directions after leaving the interstate at Tuscaloosa, until I spotted the Paul "Bear" Bryant Museum, which tempted me to stop and send my wife another postcard drawing more favorable comparisons with the Louvre. But even I had my doubts that she would know him as the legendary football coach of the Crimson Tide, who ran brutal practices in the summer heat from an Olympian tower constructed to loom over the field. Bryant had the good fortune to coach Namath, whom he called "the best athlete I have ever seen," and won several national championships and many bowl victories. While coaching, his reputation rested on his Spartan image. Namath has described one drill called Kill or Be Killed, in which three lineman would form a circle and literally fight, "kicking, slugging, anything." But a new biography examines Bryant as the popular white coach of a southern university team, caught between loyalty to school and state and the march toward desegregation, not to mention more players. He never openly confronted Governor George Wallace, but after the violence in Birmingham he did say he was thinking

< 52 >

of running for office—Bear-talk to express unhappiness with Alabama's ugly image. He only integrated the team in 1971, which hardly makes him a figure of Civil Rights importance. At the same time he understood the value of a university education in changing lives. In Bryant's own case, he got to Tuscaloosa and national fame by way of Moro Bottom, Arkansas.

The University of Alabama looks like many state universities, with red brick buildings and a quadrangle of pillared classrooms. Newer buildings surround the historic campus, as do fraternities and the mammoth football stadium, which is located where, at other colleges, you would expect to find the library. Not many people would consider the University of Alabama one of America's finer state universities, but on a spring afternoon it looked leafy and serious. Alas, its most famous football alumni, Joe Namath, has a chapter in his memoirs, "I Should Have Studied Commerce," in which he regrets his decision to major in something called Industrial Arts instead of business. That may no doubt explain some of his football-era investments, including a temporary employment agency, Mantle Men and Namath Girls, Inc., and a chain of restaurants called Broadway Joe's. But the footnote to both Namath's and Bryant's legacies is that in 2003 Joe quietly returned to the university to complete his degree in education. All that remains to be com-

< 53 >

pleted is his thesis. He refused to describe the topic to the *New York Times* but did say: "I don't want to talk about it until it's finished. Excuse me, but I don't feel good about putting off my education. I'm not proud of it one bit."

< 54 >

Oxford, Mississippi:
'let us now praise famous men'

To get to Mississippi, I drove west on Route 82, through towns named Gordo and Reform and passed signs for revival meetings proclaiming Jesus to be King. Across the state line, I took a succession of back roads toward Oxford, expecting to pass sleepy hamlets with a general store, the post office, and a church around the crossroads. I am sure that in a few places the Mississippi of *Let Us Now Praise Famous Men* still exists, but you don't see it from an air-conditioned car; at least I didn't. I found western Alabama covered with forests and rolling hills, while eastern Mississippi had more expansive farmland. Around Okolona, I realized I would be too late in Oxford to visit the Faulkner house, which I assumed closed at 5:00 p.m. But with a cell phone, I called a friend connected with the Internet, who looked up the museum and gave me the number of the director. In turn, he listened to my story and agreed to meet me at Rowan Oak, the name of

< 55 >

Faulkner's house, whenever I arrived in town. Southern hospitality survives.

I cannot say that William Griffith was delighted to interrupt his evening to show me around Faulkner's house. But he was gracious, and I was poking around the front yard when he pulled up in his truck. I am glad I persisted because there was something magical about walking alone around Rowan Oak, as if I were a weekend guest. You would think, from this determined homage, that I am a devoted Faulkner reader, there to examine the outline of *A Fable* on walls of his writing room and to compare it with the text. But the fact is I had never gotten anywhere with Faulkner. I read his short stories in high school, at a time when one writer was the same as another. In college literature classes, I found myself in study halls making no headway with *The Sound and the Fury* or *As I Lay Dying*. I wanted to like Faulkner, believed him to be an authentic voice of the South, but never managed to finish any of his books. I once had a literary friend, Joseph Epstein, write me a "How to read Faulkner" letter. But I failed with *The Hamlet*, his starter choice, replete with the Snopes in Yoknapatawpha County, which in any case I never could pronounce. For these reasons I thought seeing his house and hometown of Oxford would let me visualize words I had found so remote on paper.

Faulkner moved to Rowan Oak in 1930, when

< 56 >

he was 33 and married to Estelle Oldham Franklin, who had small children from a previous marriage. Together they later had a daughter. At the time of the move, Faulkner had published several novels (including that with the title from Shakespeare: a "*tale / told by an idiot, full of sound and fury*"), short stories, and was working on a manuscript, capturing a quote from his wife, who had noticed, "the light in August is different from any other time of year." There is a picture in the house of Faulkner typing beneath one of the grand trees in the yard. Indeed much of his work came from memory and speech—to me he is the American James Joyce. Still, it surprised me to see his small writing table, with hardly any space for books or papers. Faulkner's 2,300 books are no longer at the house, but you do see several pairs of riding boots and, leaning against the great writer's desk, a set of golf clubs. He loved horses and later in life sailed.

Omitted from the house tour is any evidence, except separate bedrooms, of Faulkner's tempestuous home life. His wife drank heavily, as did William, especially after he had finished a novel or short story, as if to purge his system. To earn money, Faulkner spent weeks away from home in Hollywood, writing movie scripts that were rarely accepted. His only major success was *The Big Sleep*. But the studios paid well, even to reject treatments. On the West Coast he could drink and find solace

< 57 >

with other women. He carried himself with a certain reserved pride, as is apparent in one anecdote told by a biographer:

> One evening he introduced Faulkner to Clark Gable, who asked the young man which writers he should be reading. Faulkner replied: "Hemingway, Cather, Mann, Dos Passos, and William Faulkner." Surprised by the last name on the list, Gable asked: "Oh, do you write?" Faulkner replied, "Yes, Mr. Gable. What do you do?"

I am not surprised that Faulkner had so little success in Hollywood. In school he was bored unless doing his own reading. He dropped out of college almost immediately after enrolling and never finished. When he worked at the Oxford post office (which he quit, famously, by saying "Thank God I won't ever again have to be at the beck and call of every son-of-a-bitch who's got two cents to buy a stamp"), he spent his time reading magazines that he failed to deliver. As a writer, he was only content telling fables of his own conception. The novelist Robert Penn Warren, who knew Faulkner, remarked: "He wasn't much of a student, not a student of other people's ideas. He had his own, and anything or anybody who got in their way was doomed to failure." Another friend remembered Faulkner: "What I best recollect are his beautiful

< 58 >

manners, his soft speech, his controlled intensity, and his astonishing capacity for hard drink."

From Rowan Oak, I drove the few blocks into Oxford to see the university, visit Square Books, and eat dinner. On most days, Faulkner would finish writing in the early afternoon and then walk into town and visit friends or his mother. He had grown up in a house located on campus. Much of Faulkner's writing can be read as either the destruction of a local family or that of the South, both of which can be glimpsed in the story involving his grandfather, who once drove around Oxford in a drunken rage until he threw a brick through the window of the bank that he owned. Explaining himself and sounding a lot like his grandson would on many later occasions, the grandfather remarked: "It was my Buick, my brick, and my bank."

My drive around Oxford was less eventful. After a few wrong turns, I found the university, a campus of visual beauty and elegant design. I expected a sprawling state university, with awkward high rises. Even though Ole Miss has a Rebel Drive and Fraternity Row, there is a gracefulness about it that does not translate from either its obsession with football or the insults hurled at James Meredith. Branch tells the story that when the CIA showed President Kennedy evidence of Soviet missiles in Cuba, he asked facetiously: "Can

< 59 >

they hit Oxford, Mississippi?" Neither John nor Robert Kennedy felt they won anything in having to send federal troops to Mississippi to enroll Meredith, even though by then they had no other choice. To Kennedy's political mind, he saw the South slipping away from the Democratic electoral bloc; in the minds of King and other civil rights advocates, federal intervention was too little and too late.

Although I was traveling light on this trip, I still bought histories, biographies, and novels at Square Books, which upstairs has a definitive collection of Faulknerania. Even without the ghost of William past, it would still be an excellent shop and is noted for attracting touring authors, especially those from the South. I ate dinner in the delightful Ajax Diner, ordering a plate that included hush puppies, cole slaw, and barbecue, not to mention a local root beer. I was tired from the long day's driving and touring, and thought of checking into one of the football motels around the town. The next day, however, I wanted to visit the battlefield at Vicksburg. To do that I would need to sleep in central Mississippi, which meant one of those after-dinner interstate drives, so familiar to anyone in sales who has ever lived off "a shoeshine and a smile."

< 60 >

Yazoo City, Mississippi:
'my dog Skip'

One of the books I acquired on the square was *North Toward Home* by Willie Morris, his memoir of growing up in Yazoo City, Mississippi, in the heart of the Delta. I remember Lewis Lapham saying that Morris's literary reputation had been based on "its first forty pages" and compared the book to Balzac's *Lost Illusions*—with irony more than affection, and then only in the sense of rural migration to big-city fame. With Morris's memoirs in hand, it occurred to me that I could spend the night in Yazoo City and then be at Vicksburg early enough to catch my flight from Jackson.

The drive from Oxford to Yazoo City (the word is of Indian origin and means "water of the dead") is more than a hundred miles, and it was close to midnight when I turned off the Interstate on to local Highway 16. On the first page of his memoirs, Morris writes: "On a quiet day after a spring rain this stretch of earth seems prehistoric—damp, cool,

< 61 >

inaccessible, the moss hanging from the giant old trees—and if you ignore the occasional diesel, churning up one of these hills on its way to Greenwood or Clarksdale or Memphis, you may feel you are in one of those sudden magic places of America, known mainly by the local people and merely taken for granted, never written about, not even on any of the tourist maps." At this hour, however, I was less interested in magical places and just wanted to find a place to spend the night. Strictly speaking, Yazoo is hardly a city, and at midnight the main street was deserted. Near the tracks and a small Amtrak station, I asked in a convenience store for hotel directions, but the clerk shrugged. I made several more loops down the main street, hoping to find the Hotel Yazoo City or something similar. I found nothing until I returned to the highway and stumbled across a motel in a shopping-center parking lot. The cost of a room was $50, and ironically the lobby rack had "tourist maps" showing the highlights of Morris's life around town.

In the morning I followed this trail of Morris's life, most of which is covered in his memoirs. Morris wrote 19 books, although the most popular was *My Dog Skip*, an account of his boyhood companion, who could both shop and play football. *North Toward Home* is divided into three sections: Morris's boyhood in Yazoo City, his college and post-graduate years in Texas, and his early years in

< 62 >

New York. Of living in rural Mississippi in the late 1940s and early 1950s, he writes: "The town in which I had grown up had yet to be touched by the great television culture, or by the hardening emotions and the defensive hostilities unloosed by the Supreme Court in 1954. Something was left, if but an oblique recollection: a Southern driftlessness, a closeness to the earth, a sense of time standing still, a lingering isolation from America's relentless currents of change and homogeneity." His childhood evokes the pages of *To Kill a Mockingbird* more than anything from Faulkner: "Almost every afternoon when the heat was not unbearable my father and I would go out to the old baseball field behind the armory to hit flies.... The smell of that new-cut grass was the finest of all smells, and I could run forever and never get tired. It was a dreamy, suspended state, those late afternoons, thinking of nothing but outfield flies as the world drifted by on Jackson Avenue." He senses the undercurrents both in the South and the town, but they are easy to ignore in a life of hunting, fishing, school dances, and sports, as he writes: "Perhaps I would have found in Faulkner some dark chord, some suggestion of how this land had shaped me, how its isolation and its guilt-ridden past had already settled so deeply in my bones. Unfortunately this was to come later. Then I joined easily and thoughtlessly in the Mississippi middle-class consensus that Faulkner,

< 63 >

the chronicler and moralist, was out for the Yankee dollar." Only later, after he had moved to New York, would Morris write: "When I was a grown man, and saw the deputy sheriffs and the mobs pummeling Negro demonstrators on television, I needed no one to tell me they had been doing the same thing since the age of eight."

Precocious at school and a gifted athlete, Morris is destined for bigger worlds than a life in Yazoo City, both at the University of Texas and afterwards as a Rhodes scholar at Oxford, England. He confesses: "But as a boy gets older, unless he has special inner resources, or a tailbone made of sheet-iron, or unless he gets saved by Billy Graham at twilight in a football stadium, the simple small-town faith starts wearing thin." He becomes editor of the University of Texas newspaper, he spends four years in Oxford, and he meets, among many others, Robert Frost. He is selected editor of *Harper's* at age 32, where among the likes of William Styron and Norman Mailer passing through his office is one William Jefferson Clinton, then out of college and on his way to Oxford. Little did Morris realize that both would share Huck Finn childhoods and Rhodes scholarships with professional achievements that were always tinged with aspects of self-destruction. Although a gifted and readable writer, Morris played the role of *enfant terrible* in American let-

< 64 >

ters, inviting confrontations that would lead to dismissals. That happened at *Harper's*, although upon reflection I doubt any editor could have sustained a relationship with John Cowles, Jr., the owner of the magazine.

< 65 >

Vicksburg, Mississippi:
'you were right and I was wrong'

The Yazoo River empties into the Mississippi above Vicksburg, and on my way southwest I drove alongside its meandering stream, wondering why it was ever such a prominent waterway. Morris writes at length about the Delta, an alluvial landscape that grew rich from the almost biblical floods of the Mississippi that washed inland. After one such flood in the Civil War, Grant sent gunboats up the Yazoo, although they bogged down in the thickets, as one history describes:

> If the trees were fewer, they were also closer together, and vermin of all kinds had taken refuge in them from the flood; so that when one of the gunboats struck a tree the quivering limbs let fall a plague of rats, mice, cockroaches, snakes, and lizards. Men were stationed about the decks with brooms to rid the vessels of such unwelcome boarders.

By Vicksburg the flatlands give way to sharper hills, clumps of forest, and, in this age, bigger highways

< 66 >

and non-descript suburban sprawl. Just after 9:00 a.m. I parked at the visitors' center of the battlefield park and browsed among the bookshelves devoted to Grant's successful siege here in 1863. Vicksburg fell to Union forces at the same time that Robert E. Lee failed to take Cemetery Ridge at Gettysburg, and no doubt these simultaneous reversals of fortune sent shudders through southern morale.

I listened to a driving-tour tape while slowly steering the car around the siege lines, which are now traversed by park roads. Here and there you see pickets of cannons, American flags, and roadside observation posts of this stockade or that redoubt. I paused reflectively when so instructed by the Park Service guiding voice, turning the tape back on when I was "done visiting Grant's headquarters area." I parked on a bluff that looked down on the Mississippi, in the positions of southern batteries that for months kept the river closed to Union naval forces. I walked around a few restored blocks of Vicksburg, which otherwise is neither an historic attraction, a railroad town, an interstate rest stop nor a center of much business, but a bland compromise of those many facets. Only after my visit did I realize the extent to which the siege of Vicksburg was an afterthought to a broader, much more interesting campaign, which lasted more than half a year and was fought along the Mississippi from well below Vicksburg north to Memphis.

< 67 >

Grant's objective along the banks of the river was to cut the Confederacy in two, and he achieved that, according to the historian Shelby Foote, on his seventh try, having failed or been defeated on the first six occasions. Only a man such as Grant, so well acquainted with failure, would have persisted.

Around New Year 1863 in Memphis, Grant received orders to take Vicksburg. He first tried both to run the batteries along the river and to strike the fortress bluffs overland. When those efforts failed, he tried to dig a canal around the west bank of the Mississippi, to speed his passage below; and he sent ironclad boats up rivers like the Yazoo and the Big Black, which gives Vicksburg the distinction of being the first battle to employ tanks—even if they floated on rivers instead of churning forward on metal treads. To win the campaign, Grant took the risk of dividing his army, as Lee did at Chancellorsville. He sent half his forces to destroy Jackson, Mississippi, while the others dug in before Vicksburg for the final siege. One history I found in the gift shop summarized this endgame: "His solution was to strike both north and east, severing the rail connection between Jackson and Vicksburg near the Big Black crossing, while simultaneously closing in on the capital. He would capture the inferior force at that place, if possible, but at any rate he would knock it out of commission as a transportation hub or a rallying

< *68* >

point; after which he would be free to turn on Vicksburg unmolested, approaching it from the east and north, and thus either take the citadel by storm or else establish a base on the Yazoo from which to draw supplies while starving the cut-off defenders into surrender."

The more I saw and read about Vicksburg, the more I imagined it to be the ideal battle to study at military academies. On the river the campaign involved important naval confrontations, artillery exchanges, and amphibious assaults. Before the city it was siege warfare, while to the north ironclads ranged inland, the way armor now supports infantry. Even civilians were engaged. It was General William T. Sherman's brigades that operated between Jackson and Vicksburg, and there he scorched the landscape as he later did while taking Atlanta—thus adding to the campaign the modernist idea of civilian terror.

Among the books I purchased in Oxford was Shelby Foote's account of Vicksburg, *The Beleaguered City*. The Modern Library published it, although the text is largely lifted from his three-volume opus on the Civil War. He later won fame as a spokesman for historical civility in the Ken Burns Civil War documentary.

Foote had tried his hand as a novelist before turning to history, which may explain the absence of academic protocol in his graceful writing. He

< 69 >

writes, for example: "Various geographic factors made Vicksburg an extremely difficult nut to crack." He is sardonic about the temperamental Sherman, quoting one account that called him "half sailor, half soldier, with a touch of the snapping turtle." Foote is amused at Sherman's obsession with hating the press. "They were so deeply laden with weighty matter that they must have sunk," is Sherman's reaction, described by Foote, when a boat carrying journalists is sent to the bottom of the river. Foote is respectful of Grant's modesty. "Somehow," he writes, Grant "was more partner than boss" in the Vicksburg campaign, and he quotes Charles Dana, who saw the failed shopkeeper-turned-general as "the most modest, the most disinterested, and the most honest man I ever knew, with a temper that nothing could disturb and judgment that was judicial in its comprehensiveness and wisdom. Not a great man except morally; not an original or brilliant man, but sincere, thoughtful, deep, and gifted with courage that never faltered." Foote ends his book with Lincoln's letter to Grant, of whom the President had earlier remarked: "I think Grant has hardly a friend left, except myself." After Vicksburg, the President writes to the general he hardly knows: "When you turned northward, east of the Big Black, I feared it was a mistake. I now wish to make the personal acknowledgement that you were right and I was wrong."

< 70 >

I was also interested to discover links among Foote and Faulkner and, indirectly, Willie Morris's Delta. Foote was born between Vicksburg and Yazoo City, alongside one of the streams contested in the battle. In the book's only footnote, he writes: "My father was born in a house later built on this mound, and was buried alongside his father in a cemetery less than a quarter of a mile away. I expect to join them there in the not–too-distant future." Foote was also a great friend of the southern novelist, Walker Percy, whose father had been host to an informal literary salon. At the house of the older Percy, Foote met William Faulkner ("who came to play tennis, but whose racket never made contact with the ball"). Like Morris, Foote grew up in the shadow of the destruction around Jackson, noting that burned plantations were called "Sherman monuments" or that their remaining chimneys were referred to as "Sherman tombstones." In *North Toward Home*, Morris's grandmother ("daughter of the editor whose printing presses had been dumped by the Yankee soldiers into the town well") inherits a sense of doom from hearing tales of the Battle of Raymond, near Jackson. Of that battle Foote quotes an observer: "There they lay, the blue and the gray intermingled; the same rich, young American blood flowing out in little rivulets of crimson; each thinking he was in the right."

< 71 >

Crawford, Texas:
'field without dreams'

On my way to Jackson, I drove through Raymond, now an exit off the interstate, and cruised past the capitol in Jackson before heading to the airport. I returned the rental car, lined up for security, removed my shoes, started my computer, extended my arms, and boarded a flight for Dallas. I was heading to Waco, more than to Dallas, and had first thought of driving or taking the train the four hundred or so miles across Louisiana and east Texas. On my 1965 train journey with my father and sister, we had gone from Mobile to New Orleans and then to Shreveport, Louisiana, which is halfway to Waco. But the passenger rail line between Mississippi and Dallas is long gone, as if Sherman's brigade had ripped up the tracks. I had also decided against another eight hours of interstate driving. In less than two hours and after an in-flight lunch of cranberry juice and peanuts, I landed in Texas at the Dallas-Fort Worth Airport, which struck me

< 72 >

as larger than many European cities.

A friend from high school, Maurice Kerins III, met me at the airport and together we drove to Waco. When I knew Maurice, he was Kerry and I was Matt. During the intervening thirty years we had kept in touch without seeing much of each other. I knew he was in Texas, but not what he was doing, until a year ago, when we found ourselves on the same e-mail correspondence list and began writing short notes to each other, usually after one of us took exception to sentiments about the need to invade Iraq. In the car leaving the labyrinthine airport, we found that we shared not only time together in school and anti-war sentiments, but banking careers. We had both been let go of our jobs under nasty circumstances, and we both loved riding racing bicycles and the Tour de France. Ironically, in that first half hour together, we had reconnected to a level of friendship that we had never had in high school.

Having seen retro-stadiums in Baltimore and Durham, I was interested to drive past the new Arlington baseball stadium, which George W. Bush had pushed both as president of the Texas Rangers and later as the state governor. Indeed Bush owed his $14-million fortune to The Ballpark at Arlington—later made famous in the movie *The Rookie*—and I was keen to see this presidential field of dreams.

< 73 >

The Ballpark, having recently sold the naming rights, is now called Ameriquest Field and was built in 1994 at a cost of $191 million. The owners of the Rangers, including George W. Bush, only had to put up $56 million. An increase in the local sales tax by one-half cent covered a $135-million public bond issue that paid for the rest. But after only $60 million in interest and principal were repaid, ownership of the stadium reverted to the Rangers. Suddenly a second-division team, with sparse attendance, owned a lavish new stadium halfway between Fort Worth and Dallas—with both a picnic area and an office building in centerfield. The team that Bush and his partners bought for less than $100 million was suddenly worth over $200 million. Bush was the Texas governor when the team was sold in 1998 for $250 million. To show gratitude to the governor and potential presidential candidate for all he had done for the Rangers, his partners later voted him stock options that transformed an initial investment of less than $1 million into a return of almost $15 million. On top of all that, the buyer of the team, Tom Hicks, had made a fortune from the state by managing the investments of various Texas educational trust funds—for a system that failed to graduate 50 percent of its students from city high schools. At least when Babe Ruth made more money than the president, he had had a better year.

< 74 >

Maurice could not cross about six lanes of highway traffic so we missed both the stadium and the interstate south to Waco. Instead, because we had time, we decided to drive south on back roads and stop in Crawford, where Bush has his ranch. I had assumed that the Bush homestead, Prairie Chapel, was near Austin, but it is about twenty miles northwest of Waco. We escaped the traffic and urban sprawl around Dallas and followed a two-lane blacktop road that rolls through lovely hill country closer to Crawford. Willie Morris traveled around the state as a young reporter for the *Texas Observer*, recalling: "I traveled all over Texas, from one end to the other, and my memory of it as a physical presence is like a montage, with brilliant lights and furious machinery in the background, and in the foreground a country café with old men in front, watching big cars speed by."

Crawford, alas, does not even have a café. I confess I was stunned by the nothingness of it. Down one side are a few stores, the proverbial Bush souvenir shop, and a police station. Across the street all I saw were a grain elevator and train tracks. The sign proclaiming the presence of the western White House would hardly dignify the sale of used cars missing engines. Bush's ranch, however, is eight miles from town. We did not try to find it, assuming we would be turned back long before we saw something looking like Southfork. We

< 75 >

speculated how state visits or any kind of govern-ment could be managed in the middle of nowhere, as if in Bedouin tents. In the tumbleweed fields of Crawford, I sensed some of Bush's contempt for public discourse—an impression anti-war protester Cindy Sheehan may have formed during her own stay in town.

< 76 >

Branch Davidian Texas:
'devouring our own'

I found it impossible to be in Waco and not to try to visit the world of David Koresh that Attorney General Janet Reno had reduced to ashes. In another version of this history, it was Koresh himself who put his own parish to the torch. But the few people that I asked about the Branch Davidian house didn't know exactly where it was located. It was only late in the day that I met a Baylor professor of journalism, Sara Whelan, who was willing to track down its location. She had recently moved to Waco from New Orleans, and thus she still had a newcomer's curiosity. We stopped at an interstate tourist office, and a few minutes later Professor Whelan proudly emerged from the building with pre-printed directions to "Mount Carmel," the formal name of the building complex that, in April 1993, burned to the ground after officers from the Federal Bureau of Investigation (FBI) and the Bureau of Alcohol, Firearms, and Tobacco (ATF) moved in with tanks and nerve gas.

< 77 >

In trying to find the Double EE Rand Road on lonesome prairie, we made a few wrong turns and actually pulled into the driveway of the Double EE Ranch, which is as impressive as any described in Edna Ferber's *Giant*. A ranch hand corrected our mistake—we had turned left one road too early—and in a few moments we parked Whelan's car on the edge of Mt. Carmel, in front of a makeshift museum that had a hand-painted sign offering tours of the grounds for $5. A few hundred yards into the property is a newly built white church. Between the road and its front door there are rows of freshly planted trees and small headstones, memorializing the names of the 81 Davidians who died in the 1993 firefights. In effect, the Koresh church still owns or controls the land, although title is contested within the sect. It is used partly for the congregation and partly as a parable on freedom of religion and government violence.

If, when I had stood in the drive of the Koresh estate, I had been asked to recount the events that had defined the first year of the Bill Clinton presidency, I would have said trigger-happy members of the FBI and ATF had attacked a rural commune—one that worshipped polygamy and guns as much as the second coming of Christ. I believed Attorney General Reno had used what is called "excessive force," but I knew nothing about the cult's leader, David Koresh, other than sensing that he and his

< 78 >

followers had gotten their wish of having their judgment day coincide with a fiery conflagration. But mostly I would have been guessing, not having seen any of the siege on television, and never having read any histories of either Koresh or his followers. Nevertheless, standing in the Texas sunshine, I believed Mt. Carmel to be a variation on the themes of Jonestown, only this time the ATF had spiked the Kool Aid.

A few weeks later, after leaving Waco, I read several histories of the 1993 barn burning. In Waco itself, the local Barnes & Noble had no books on either Koresh or his demise. (The city would prefer more positive associations.) But from the Internet I purchased *The Ashes of Waco: An Investigation* by Dick J. Reavis, which from reading the promotional quotes I hoped might be free from the many conspiracy theories that this Armageddon has inspired. From Reavis, I was finally able to connect the grounds on which we parked Whelan's car to the events of winter and spring 1993. Alas, the museum promising $5 tours was closed, and the Mt. Carmel church doors were locked. And there were no pilgrims on the road. Thus we walked the grounds in eerie silence, as if on a movie set that had lost its audio feed.

* * *

To give a bare minimum of the church's background, it is necessary to start by saying that David

< 79 >

Koresh was his adopted biblical name, and that the leader of the Branch Davidians (not a name the group used to describe itself) was born Vernon Howell. He grew up in a broken Texan home, his mother having been 14 when he was born and his father absent from his life. Long before Howell drifted to Waco in 1980, the rural complex of wooden buildings had been associated with a schismatic group of Seventh-Day Adventists. Reavis calls them "perhaps renegade, but heirs nonetheless" of the "eight-million member Seventh-Day Adventist (SDA) Church," which, can count among its early believers John Harvey Kellogg, the father of corn flakes. In 1942, a splinter group had renamed itself the "Davidian Seventh Day Adventist Association," and it was from a lease in that name on Mt. Carmel lands that the press got the notion that Koresh's followers should be known as "Branch Davidians."

In fact, textual inspiration for the Koresh faithful came from the Seven Seals in the Book of Revelation, and those living at Mt. Carmel—a potluck of communal Europeans, Australians, and Americans—would have thought themselves nothing more exotic than students of the Bible, with emphasis on the Seven Seals. Although some of the men trained with firearms, it was not a gun cult, as you would find in rural Montana. Indeed, Reavis writes: "The people who had lived at Mt. Carmel were more akin to the Shakers and to the Onieda

< 80 >

community—parts of today's Americana—than to the members of the Charles Manson cult." But if all they were doing out there on the Double EE Ranch Road was reading the Bible or baking bread, how did it come to pass that they found themselves under siege by the combined arms of the FBI, the ATF, and the National Guard?

In reality, the G-men were attacking David Koresh more than they were laying waste to a rural congregation, near nothing and no one, 12 miles outside the city of Waco. Deserved or not, he had gained a reputation among local law-enforcement officials as a new-age preacher who was dredging up quotations from the New Testament to justify polygamy, dope dealing, and the stockpiling of assault rifles. In 1992 a UPS man had sounded the alarm after he spotted some hand grenades at the church.

Koresh had become a marked man. While thundering in his pulpit, he had found time to father 17 children, some with girls under the legal age of consent and others by women married to fellow Davidians. He had also amassed a formidable gun collection, notably from a co-religionist who made the rounds of the Texas gun shows. Although a man of the cloth—he told his flock that he was a third Christ, "a mortal embodying the spirit of God"—Koresh enjoyed jamming with a communal rock band long into Texas summer

< 81 >

nights. Had the Davidians not been armed, the encampment might well have seemed an outtake from *Life of Brian*. (Brian's mother: "He's not the Messiah. He's a very naughty boy.") In the makeshift cemetery in front of the rebuilt Mt. Carmel church is the wreckage of a Harley Davidson, a Koresh favorite when he wasn't preaching about the "investigative Judgment of the dead." One of his followers recalled: "David didn't read anything but the Bible and Camaro magazines."

In retrospect, had local police officials wanted either to question or to arrest Koresh (although being a Messiah is not a crime in Texas or anywhere else), all they needed to do was pick him up on one of his frequent trips into Waco. The residents of Mt. Carmel may have had their own views on the Book of Revelation, not to mention their special take on marriage laws, but they did come and go from their compound. Instead the ATF cooked up one of those police raids that you see on television when it is airing "Real Tales from the Highway Patrol" or covering some narcotics bust.

At around 10:00 a.m. on February 28, various law-enforcement officers, backed up by armed helicopters, tried to overrun Mt. Carmel. Standing at the front door, Koresh was badly wounded in the initial assault. But in an amazing feat of arms (no matter which side of this story you believe), the Davidian militia fought off the ATF raiders,

< *82* >

including the armed helicopters that had strafed the church buildings. Twenty attackers were wounded, and four were killed. The Davidians suffered six killed. In a truce negotiated over the phone, the government withdrew from the property and laid down its siege lines, which isolated the compound for almost two months. Hence began the Texas standoff that attracted more than 1,000 members of the world media, not to mention the FBI and U.S. Army brass, including those in General Wesley Clark's chain of command, who would later supply the assault armor.

On April 19, under rules of engagement signed by Attorney General Reno, the government attacked again, this time using tanks to pierce the Mt. Carmel Center's walls and to shoot canisters of CS nerve gas into the wooden compound. (As the tanks rolled forward, an FBI public address system blared: "This is not an assault. This is not an assault.") Not reassured, the Davidians fought the mechanized agents, although this time the buildings caught fire and consumed all but nine of the 84 residents, including 21 children under age 16. From these ashes have come the conspiracy theories, many of which dwell on who started the fatal fire.

In the accounts of the U.S. and state governments, Koresh devoured his own, as if fulfilling a prophesy in the Book of Revelation, rather than

< 83 >

submit to the laws of civil society. Other histories, however, explain how CS nerve gas can become combustible, especially when shot by a tank into a wooden building. None of the nine Davidian survivors saw the fire start. But there is agreement that Koresh had the corridors at Mt. Carmel lined with hay, either as part of its primitive defense network or to feed the flames of judgment day.

In weighing the evidence against Koresh, Reavis, who has been a Nieman Fellow at Harvard University and who was an editor at *Texas Monthly*, disputes much official testimony. He quotes numerous witnesses to say that Koresh did not deal in drugs, and he cites the FBI itself to confirm that child abuse was not a variant at Mt. Carmel. Uncomfortably, he also reminds readers that "there is no federal or Texas statute against stockpiling arms; anyone who can legally buy one weapon can legally buy a hundred, or even a thousand of them." He describes Koresh the progenitor and Koresh the gunsmith as inhabiting legal worlds of his own construction, backed up by odd quotes from the Bible. (He once described Mt. Carmel's extraterritorial status with a reference to Vatican City.) But the Waco story lays bare all sorts of troubling constitutional issues about freedom of religion, the right to bear arms, what constitutes a church, private property, and the uses of federal troops to enforce state laws. Is it biblical or state law

< 84 >

that should govern what goes on in the backseat of a Camaro?

As the church doors were locked and the museum was closed, there wasn't much to see on the grounds of Mt. Carmel. Near the church are the burned remains of a bus and numerous headstones, just as you would find on a battlefield. We lingered over the marker that reads: "In remembrance of all the men, women and children who were victimized and brutally slaughtered in the bombing of the Oklahoma City Federal Building on April 19, 1995. We pray that they and their families find comfort and peace in Our Lord."

Two years to the day after Mt. Carmel burned, Timothy McVeigh detonated the explosives in his rented Ryder truck in anger over what he perceived as government-sponsored murder of the Davidians. During the initial siege at Waco, McVeigh had even tried to get close to Mt. Carmel and, while near the barricades, had passed out leaflets that read: "A Man With A Gun Is A Citizen, A Man Without A Gun Is A Subject." But I still find it difficult to decode the symbolism of this monument, placed where it is. Is it just condemning all random violence or acts of terror? Does it imply indirect sympathy with McVeigh, who believed that ATF officers were at work in the Alfred P. Murah Building in Oklahoma City? In a larger sense, all

< 85 >

the monuments in front of the church, including those placed by the ATF, raise the difficult question about who are the victims at Waco: the dead government officers, the Davidian women and children, or the U.S. Constitution?

Leaving Mt. Carmel, Professor Whelan and I stopped at the only other house on the road and chatted at length with a man who for years had been David Koresh's next-door neighbor. I never did learn his name, but during the siege the FBI had taken over his house—and only months later had paid him compensation. He now regretted that he had come to live across the street from a cult, and he told the story of how late one night, a family had escaped from Koresh's heavy-handed control and asked the neighbor to drive them into town, which he did. The next morning, when an angry Koresh confronted him about hustling away these wayward sheep, the neighbor played it coolly dumb, saying: "But, David, I thought you had wanted me to take them into town." His feeling was that Koresh, himself, had ignited the last fire, but he hardly believed the Davidians a threat to anyone but themselves. He and his wife had kept a polite distance from the commune, which often acted as though the Messiah had returned as Led Zeppelin. The rock music annoyed the neighbors more than the guns or the Bible classes. (What house in Texas isn't stockpiled with

< 86 >

rifles and Bibles?) And the neighbor could well be the source of a quote in Reavis: "I'll tell you what does bother me. This is a big fuss over nothing. These people have been here a long time and never bothered nobody."

< 87 >

Waco, Texas:
'ranchers and people who own a ranch'

That night in Waco, Maurice and I had dinner with
Bernard Rapoport, a philanthropist and
Democratic-party contributor to many campaigns,
and Molly Ivins, who writes a nationally syndicated
column and who is the author of a number of
books, including several biographies of George W.
Bush. At dinner, in conversation about Crawford,
Molly Ivins said Texans make an important distinction between people who ranch, and those
who own ranches. But then she told one of the
clean little secrets about Prairie Chapel, which is
that Bush is a closet environmentalist, despite his
skepticism about global warming. For hot water
and the like, the ranch has solar paneling and
ample recycling. It was also apparently built to
maintain harmony with the landscape, at odds
with the impression, which Bush feeds, that his
vacation house is a place to cut down trees or perhaps spud oil wells. The land is leased to neigh-
boring ranchers, but Molly made no mention of

< 88 >

free-range chickens or hot houses planted with arugala.

In every way the dinner that evening was felicitous. I had corresponded with B Rapoport, as he is known, for several years, but we had never met. In fact, I knew little about him until I wrote a review of *Bushwacked* by Molly Ivins, whom I also had not known, and found a profile of Rapoport in the book. She describes him as one of the few wealthy persons she admires and recounted not just his success in the insurance business, but his charitable contributions and love of books, which is how I got to know him. For years he had sent books to the chairman of the bank where I worked, and I had read some of this collection, always admiring his choices. To say thank you, I later sent him my own book, and that's how our friendship began. In planning my cross-country journey, I decided it would be worth a detour to Waco to meet him, and it was. B, in turn, invited Molly Ivins to the dinner, and all of us went to the Waco Country Club and ate dinner at a table overlooking the golf course, where sometimes Bush comes to play and, no doubt, to replace his divots.

It is impossible not to like or admire B Rapoport. His father emigrated from Riga, Latvia, to the United States in 1913, but the boat diverted from Ellis Island to Galveston. His father supported his family by selling goods from a pushcart in

San Antonio. He describes his father as the only socialist living in Texas at the time and says he would wake up his son with the cheerful, "Workers of the world, unite!" B had polio as a child, and, although he recovered, he spent a long year largely bedridden, where his companions were books from the public library. Even today in his 88th year—according to friends like Molly—he is often awake at 5:00 a.m. to read books and mark passages. Before dinner he showed me his library. Many wealthy people have collections of leather-bound classics, most of which remain unread. But B's books all look to have been read, and they float around his house the way the books of college professors end up on radiators. Indeed, B dreamed of becoming a university professor after attending the University of Texas. But he started working in insurance, found he could both sell policies and hire good people, and during his lifetime created a fortune, much of which, I infer, he would like now to give to charitable or other causes. In 1972, he met Bill Clinton, who was then organizing the campaign in Texas for George McGovern. In 1991 B was the first contributor to Clinton's own campaign, but later scoffed at the idea of becoming an ambassador and having to leave Waco.

Naturally the talk over dinner often turned to politics. Molly Ivins can tell stories as well as she can write. She has a soft voice, but almost a

< 90 >

stage presence when she speaks, and a wonderful inflexion during her punch lines. Sadly I did not write down any of the stories she told, and the only one I can now remember involves Robert Shrum, the Democratic operative who had managed the campaign of John Kerry. I questioned his political batting average, wondering if he had not gone something like 0-for-8 in presidential campaigns. It prompted Molly to defend him, and she recalled being with Shrum while a group of them were watching Bill Clinton campaign in 1992. The Arkansas governor had just gone through a long recital about how his father was an alcoholic, how his mama had raised him, and how his brother had been tormented, when a Republican operative turned to Shrum and said: "Well, he's got the dysfunctional-family vote, it seems." Without missing a beat, according to Molly, Shrum answered: "Oh, really, are the Reagans voting for him?"

A lot of the evening was spent discussing the *Texas Observer*, a liberal weekly that B supports financially and for which Molly contributes a column. It discouraged both of them that, in a state of 20 million people, in which Democratic candidates often win elections, the liberal magazine only had 8,000 subscribers. In the 1960s, back from his Rhodes scholarship in England, Willie Morris had spent several years on an earlier incarnation of the *Observer*. In *North Toward Home* he tells of spending

< 91 >

time swilling bourbon with state legislators, one of whom confesses: "You know, a politician's got to sell out to somebody, it's just a matter of pickin' the right people to sell out to. I've sold out to the truckers and to liquor. I may be their property, but I have never yet cast a vote against the people. The truckers aren't a bad group, and the good thing about the liquor boys is that when you vote for the truckers when you really don't want to, you can go off and get drunk about it free of charge."

After dinner we all said good-bye in a parking lot (it was Texas after all), and Maurice and I drove to his home in Dallas. He had been without work for a year and was thinking of selling his house. It was a beautiful house, with a large kitchen and a friendly dog that ambled around the guest room. But what I admired most about Maurice was that, despite a hard year of unemployment and job searching, he was back in graduate school studying advanced mathematics and statistics. His banking work had got him interested in the probability of risk, and to understand it better he thought he needed either a masters or a Ph.D. in mathematics, something he was working toward at a university in Dallas. I remembered that after high school Maurice had gone to college at Swarthmore, one of America's elite schools, if you read the college guides. But what impressed me about his curriculum now was his passion to learn—not just to

< 92 >

graduate with a degree from an expensive university. It is what I want for my children, starting with Helen: not a particular college, not a university pedigree, but an education that might someday—when one of the children is fifty and having a bad year (my own circumstances on this trip)—send them back to the company of books and professors, perhaps one with the sparkle of B Rapoport.

The next morning, after carefully inspecting his bicycle, Maurice and I toured his neighborhood and talked about real-estate prices, investment probabilities, American revolutionary-era histories, and newspapers. On the way to the airport, he stopped the car in Dealey Plaza, where President Kennedy was assassinated, so that we could walk off the Grassy Knoll and exchange theories about second gunmen and the Zapruder film, running continuously upstairs in the Book Depository museum. I recounted seeing President Kennedy a month before he went to Dallas, when I was nine and he was dedicating a library at Amherst College in Massachusetts. His motorcade had driven down the main street of that university town, and Kennedy had been sitting on the back of an open convertible, as if this were the homecoming parade. I remember the shock of his red hair and toothy smile, but also a premonition of his vulnerability, apparent then even to a nine-year-old boy. Nothing marks Dealey Plaza as the place where the

< 93 >

President was killed. Even the small museum is a commercial venture. Forty years later, it is difficult to comprehend the attitude in Dallas toward the assassination: Embarrassment? Indifference? Civic pride? In the car Maurice and I talked about the Oswalds in Russia, a profile of Marina in the *New Yorker*, the Fair Play for Cuba Committee, the CIA and the Mafia, Jack Ruby, Oliver Stone, and then in one of those airport rushes we said good-bye, and I was off to Los Angeles.

< 94 >

Los Angeles:
'here's to you, Mrs. Robinson'

My seat was on the right side of the plane, next to the window, and I had hopes of seeing the Rockies, maybe even figuring out which mountain passes might work best on a bicycle. But cloud covered the ground after about Midland, Texas, and only cleared when we descended below the haze over LAX.

I arrived with car and hotel reservations, but also the feeling that Los Angeles would be strange to me. My only sustained time here was in January 1973, when I spent a month as a volunteer for Cesar Chavez's United Farm Workers. As part of the lettuce boycott, I stood in front of Safeway supermarkets, urging people not to buy produce or, when that plea wore thin, something called Australian bull meat. Others had done the driving, and the different neighborhoods in Los Angeles had always looked the same, especially the Safeway parking lots. This time I doubted I would find my

< 95 >

way around. But once I had my rental car, I followed directions to turn left onto Crenshaw Boulevard and, to my surprise, immediately felt at home. I avoided the freeways, cut back and forth on streets that came slowly back into memory, and pulled up in front of my Hollywood hotel as if I had been in a taxi.

I loved everything about the Hotel Roosevelt, which I picked both because it was on Hollywood Boulevard and because the first Academy Awards were held in its ballroom. Friends had told me that Hollywood was seedy and full of tourists, but I found that part of the appeal. Most of the year I live in the Swiss countryside and wake up to a neighbor's rooster. It was a pleasure to check into a hotel that had valet parking, slightly off-beat rooms, an elegant lobby, and only cost $120 a night. I never did get across the street to look at the sidewalk in front of Grauman's Chinese restaurant. But that's because it looked like a complicated drive.

That first afternoon I had business meetings arranged, but they fell apart in West Coast fashion. Every time I would confirm the meeting, some time later the secretary would call me back to suggest other options, which in another hour she would cancel. In the end, I was told the person I was to meet had left town. Thus I was free for the late afternoon. For a while I had hopes of seeing the J. Paul Getty Museum, but it was on the wrong side

< 96 >

of the city for my dinner, and even in LA you can't have it all. Instead I drove to the home of a friend from high school and filled in the last twenty years of our lives.

During the course of the conversation. my friend, Kevin Glynn, invited me to observe his classes the following morning at LA High School. I accepted. I had known he was teaching, but unaware that it was in a central-city high school, the kind that in made-for-TV movies usually has gang fights. Kevin teaches advanced placement American history and social studies and said if I could get there by 7:37 a.m. the next morning, I was free to attend his classes. He sketched directions on my map, but as most of Los Angeles is a grid, it is easy to get around. The next day I found the school without trouble and even left the car alongside MacArthur Park, where someone left that cake out in the rain.

LA High has 5,000 students, of whom 70 percent are Latino, 10 percent are African-American, and the rest are white and what Kevin called "other." By that he meant students literally from around the world. During the course of the morning I met a girl from Sri Lanka (she had a flower in her hair), another from Mongolia, and a number of Koreans. I had expected metal detectors at the front door, and a gangs of LA atmosphere in the halls. When it was redesigned in the 1970s, LA

< 97 >

High acquired the fortified look of a prison, a concrete façade with turret-like openings, as Kevin quipped, so that "they can't throw the teachers out of the window." But I found the school relaxed. Near the principal's office are pictures of famous graduates, who include the O. J. Simpson lawyer, Johnny Cochran, and the actor Dustin Hoffman, who was actually 30 when he appeared in *The Graduate* as Benjamin Braddock ("Oh no, Mrs. Robinson. I think you're the most attractive of all my parents' friends. I mean that.") At the time, Anne Bancroft was 36. Kevin told me the high school, despite its central-city image, was also famous for its marching band, which appears regularly in the Rose Bowl parade.

I have liked and admired Kevin since the 1960s, so of course I think he is an excellent teacher. In high school, for our senior project, he and I cooked up the idea to study coal mining in West Virginia. For two weeks in the spring of 1972, we rode trains and buses, and hitchhiked around the coalfields. A few miners even showed us the mine shafts, and in Hundred, West Virginia, with no more hotels than Yazoo City, the sheriff let us sleep in the town jail. After college at Colgate, Kevin served as an officer in the Navy. When leaving active duty in the early 1990s, he had the idea that he might like to teach. He got his teaching credential in California and then his position at LA High. From his letters, I

< 98 >

recalled that he had once broken up an ugly gang fight, and took some licks in the process, but that only reminded me how he had never suffered bullies in any schoolyard. He said he had not had gang problems since then. Indeed LA High looked a lot like the high schools I know in Switzerland, where the classrooms have bare walls and the grounds around the school offer few frills. But he spoke of LA not in the context of a central-city high school, but more as a melting pot of immigrant dreams.

Kevin was teaching Watergate to his American history class when I arrived. In short segments, probably the length of an MTV video, he could hold the class's attention on such questions as Deep Throat and the missing 18 minutes on President Nixon's tapes. Then, collectively, the students' attention would wander: some of the girls would flip through *Cosmo*, others would check their cell phones for messages, and a few would stroll around until Kevin plunged ahead on the point that Nixon would have been impeached had he not resigned. I admired his ability to gauge the temperament of the class and how he knew when to enforce order and when to keep students engaged with humor. As it happened, Kevin and I had been together in an AP history class in 1972. For whatever reasons, ours had been a class that could sit silently for an hour while Mr. O'Hanlon would lecture on George

< 99 >

Kennan and the origins of the containment policy. But I know that style of teaching is from another age, like the ties we wore to school. Now professors need to have a lot of Jerry Springer in their approach—"So how do you feel about the invasion of Cambodia?"—and school children are more like audiences, there to be entertained.

During a break, I asked the class how many of them planned to go to college. Nearly everyone raised a hand, which astounded me. Admittedly, this was an Advanced Placement class, but I still found the large percentage surprising. In Switzerland, only a handful of students go to university. My daughter is one of two from her primary school class still on a university track. Others who fail to make the grade are shunted into vocational training or technical schools. But here at LA High, where a number of kids seemed to have rudimentary reading and writing skills, many were finding places in the state university system. One boy I met, Michael Lichtenstein, had been accepted at Georgetown. (When we spoke, Kevin teased him playfully: "Please meet our only black Republican." But clearly Michael's achievements were a pride of the school.) Later, when Kevin walked me around the buildings, he despaired about the bias in California to spend so much money on universities like Berkeley and to put so little money into central-city high schools. At one point he said off-handedly: "When I hear about a new auditorium at UCLA, I think: Wait a minute, I need a new chair."

Late in the morning I left LA High. I had a business lunch in Glendale, for which I arrived at 12:30 p.m. Again, for whatever reasons—although I blame bad karma—we actually started eating at 3:15 p.m. and I had to spend the waiting time in a windowless conference room without a phone. For the rest of the day, indeed for the rest of my stay in the land of Lotus, I cruised. I ate sushi in the hills above Brentwood and had dinner at a country club near Pasadena. I went by the condo where O. J.'s wife and her friend Ron Goldman were murdered (the new owners have replanted the garden and I suppose raked over the Bruno Magli shoeprints), and I drove by Chavez Ravine, the home of the Los Angeles Dodgers, who were lured away from Brooklyn with the promise of a new stadium.

I even found the house in which I had lived in January 1973. At first I only remembered that it was near Western and Washington boulevards. After that I recalled it was on South Hobart, and then I remembered the street number, 23, and recognized the house, which has since been turned into a day-care center. When I lived there, it was a student crash pad. Everyone slept on the floor in sleeping bags and ate communal meals in the evenings. It was close enough to Watts that we rarely went walking at night, but now the

< 101 >

neighborhood is largely Korean. During our free, non-lettuce-boycotting time, we played basketball in Pauley Pavilion on the UCLA campus and drove to Santa Barbara to watch the sunset. Back on the picket line, we all enjoyed the Safeways in Santa Monica and Venice Beach, especially when approaching cars proclaiming solidarity with whales and rain forests. In one encounter, I had a near-endless conversation with a member of the 1960s rock group, the Chi-Lites ("Have You Seen Her?"), who then had exactly the same conversation with some of my fellow boycotters. The singer came back many days and would end each rap by announcing: "Tell your friend he's been schooled by an entertainer." I remember leaving LA a month after asking everyone, "Where's downtown?" and never feeling I ever got there.

< 102 >

San Francisco:
'east toward home'

Officially my cross-country tour did not end in Los Angeles. From Burbank, I flew to San Jose and visited with family and friends in Palo Alto and San Francisco. In the Bay Area, I convinced my godson, Joe Street, to walk me around the new Pac Bell Stadium, home of the San Francisco Giants, where the backwater beyond the right-field fence is known as McCovey Cove. We bought souvenirs and discussed whether the records of Barry Bonds should be erased if it was proven he had taken the juice. But mostly I ate more sushi, visited with family, and admired Bay Area gentility. For excitement, one night I awoke and looked out on the street to discover that a romantic couple had triggered the car alarm during their passion, and now a policeman had arrived and was shining one of those long-barreled flashlights into the compromised backseat. On the way to the Oakland airport—before I flew

< 103 >

home to Europe—my brother-in-law detoured to show me the boarding house in Berkeley where in *The Graduate* Ben rents a room, hoping to catch glimpses of Elaine Robinson. (About this time his mother asks: "What makes you think she wants to marry you?" To which Benjamin replies: "Oh, she doesn't. To be perfectly honest she doesn't like me.") Near the airport we passed Oakland-Alameda County Stadium, the longtime home to the football Oakland Raiders, and so unfashionable that fans referred to it as the Black Hole—the anti-Christ to the revivalist sentiments spawned in Camden Yards.

Flying back to Europe, I reflected how little cut American grass I had actually smelled. Except for the Civil War battlefields, I had not set foot in a national park, and my only train ride was two hours on Amtrak between Trenton and Baltimore. I had missed New Orleans, and cloud had covered much of the Rockies. I had not gone west so much as whistle-stopped between old friends. But perhaps the best measure of the trip is that I never felt tired, not even on the red eye out of Oakland. I had slept fitfully in guest rooms, hotels, and that motel in Yazoo City, but never awoke feeling as I do when the alarm rings for work. I had liked Mississippi more than I expected, and during the course of my travels, I had put together a virtual high school reunion. Even at the Oakland airport, I had seen a

< 104 >